YOU CAN'T LOSE IF THE CUSTOMER WINS

YOU CAN'T LOSE IF THE CUSTOMER WINS

Ten Steps to Service Success

Ronald A. Nykiel

Longmeadow Press

To my wife Karen, our son Ron, Jr.,
and my friends in the service industry.
A special thanks to Irene
for her help in this endeavor.

Copyright © 1990 by Ronald A. Nykiel

Cover design by Art Patrol/NYC

Interior design by Barbara Cohen Aronica

ISBN: 0-681-41023-X

Printed in the United States of America
0 9 8 7 6 5 4 3 2

CONTENTS

PREFACE

The past 20 years have produced a consumer grown increasingly cynical. The easy and oft-cited explanation for this cynicism is that it is a symptom of our current society—the result of deterioration in our institutions. Scandals and wrongdoings in the church, government and the stock exchange have contributed to consumer cynicism.

However, there are other reasons why consumers are cynical. After all, not many consumers roaming the aisles of local stores are absorbed in thought about scandals involving television evangelists, crooked politicians, or Wall Street scams. In fact, many do not attend church, do not give a damn about politics, and do not own stocks.

The source of consumer cynicism as it relates to the service industries in America is more complex. Sure, societal issues and the general mood are partial causes. However, a closer examination of the preservice economy reveals an already full-blown consumer cynicism—a cynicism that has resulted from experiences with manufactured goods. As prices increased with high inflation during the third quarter of this century, the quality of products decreased in virtually all categories. The consumer has experienced everything from recalled autos to tainted canned foods.

So, enter the service sector, which has been emerging in its own right, at the height of this consumer awareness and cynicism aimed at institutions and manufactured products. It has bred a new force in society—the professional skeptic and cynic—acting as watchdog for the public at large. In short, this is neither the best time to be offering a service, nor is it the best environment in which to become successful in so doing.

On the other hand, what better time to distinguish one's service than now—by overcoming consumer cynicism through positive performance? In reviewing the literature on how to achieve service success, and even overcome consumers' cynical attitudes and behavior patterns, I found what I will refer to as "event" or "experience" examples. These are actual experiences described by the people involved or who observed others involved. I read of an airline that realized if it treated its employees better, the employees would, in turn, treat its passengers better. I read of a bank that extended its hours and outlets. I read of a carpet cleaning service that will run a white towel across your carpet to prove that it is clean—and will clean it again if it is not.

What I could not find was a simple "how to" approach for recognizing and addressing the actual cynicism of the consumer. Thus, while I make reference to some examples culled from experience, I shall focus on the processes of achieving successful service and changing cynical behavior. I shall then go beyond these steps and deal with the all-important processes of communication and perception.

In essence, making your service business successful is what this book is all about.

ACKNOWLEDGMENTS

During my years in the service industry, I have been fortunate to meet and learn from many people: first, the hundreds of reservationists, front-desk clerks, bellmen, stewardesses, waiters and waitresses, and others who have demonstrated an attitude and professionalism that helped overcome my cynicism; next, the industry leaders who provided me with the opportunity to learn more about service or, as the old Marriott ad campaign said, "When we do it, we do it right!" Thank you, Bill Marriott (Chairman, Marriott Corporation), and Juergen Bartels (President, Carlson Hospitality Companies), for the personal examples you provided. Thank you Jan Carlson (President, SAS) for writing *Moments of Truth,* and Frank Lorenzo (Chairman, Continental Air Corporation), for the lunch in New York that led to the idea for this book. Also, thank you Jim Biggar (Chairman and CEO, Nestle Enterprises, Inc.), and Bill Hulett (President, Stouffer Hospitality Group), whose philosophy of "Only the very best" in product quality and service standards provided further positive examples.

I

The Age
of
Cynicism

SETTING MYSELF UP

It was 5:45 A.M. and I was leaving my east side suburban Cleveland home to catch a 7:30 A.M. USAir flight to New York's LaGuardia. I usually leave home early, never knowing how bad the traffic will be on the seven-mile stretch of Brookpark Road that had served as the last link of I–480 between the east and west sides of Cleveland. (I say "had" served, since the last link of the interstate has taken more than 25 years to complete as a result of politics, law suits, funding, and who knows what else and has just recently been opened to traffic.)

With United's cutback in service and the disappearance of New York Air, there was only one other choice to LaGuardia—another USAir flight, but that wouldn't arrive until 11:16 A.M. and I had a noon lunch appointment, which there would be no chance of making in New York traffic, even if the plane arrived on time. Anyway, the 7:30 flight gave me an opportunity to call on Hertz, which was cutting back their service commitment to my company's hotels. I needed a face-to-face meeting to determine their true intent with regard to honoring our contract.

It was a good thing I left home early. A truck had broken down and traffic was backed up. Arriving at the airport, I headed for the short-term lot and parked in the first available space that was convenient to the terminal entrance. I parked in the lot in spite of my doubts that the car would still be there when I returned that evening. (The number of cars that are stolen from that lot has always amazed me.) Seeing that the sun was coming out, I left my umbrella in the car and ran for my flight.

I arrived at LaGuardia in a heavy downpour but on time (only 10 minutes late is considered "on time" at that airport) and near the end of rush hour. After spending several minutes in line at the men's room, I proceeded past the long cab lines downstairs to the upper deck drop-off area hoping to grab a cab there. Within seconds, a cabbie picked me up (illegally). As I left the airport, I glanced down at the long line of rain-soaked, irritated travelers still waiting for the dispatcher to move the equally irritated cabbies.

The tunnel was backed up (according to the traffic reports), so we opted for the back streets of Queens and the 59th Street Bridge. When we reached the Hertz offices in midtown, the cabbie told me the fare was $28.50. Since I had taken this cab ride frequently, the fare seemed high. In answer to my protests, I was informed of a recent 22% rate hike. I paid and headed for the office building in search of a men's room so I could dry off before going to the meeting.

The meeting went as expected: uneventful and unpromising. I admit, however, that I was not fully concentrating on the discussion—I was anticipating the lunch to which I had been invited that was to be held in The Boardroom, seven or eight blocks away. It started to rain as I walked to 48th and Park, and with regret I remembered the umbrella I had decided to leave behind. (And where was a street vendor when you needed one?) When it began to pour heavily, I took shelter under the overhang of the Colgate Building at 300 Park. I disconsolately thought, it isn't even noon and already I am tired, sweaty, and rain-soaked. In a few minutes I was going to have lunch with Frank

Lorenzo, then Chairman of Texas Air Corporation. The lunch was either a recruiting effort or simply a "thank you" for some kind remarks I had made about Lorenzo in a recent speech. Not knowing the reason made it seem all the more important.

Following an enjoyable lunch, Mr. Lorenzo asked about my plan for the return trip to Cleveland. I had my ticket for USAir's 5:59 flight from LaGuardia, but when I indicated I might catch an earlier flight, he generously offered to have his secretary schedule a reservation on the 2:51 Continental flight from Newark. After checking my watch, I said I'd go for it. Quickly I caught a cab and asked, "How much to Newark Airport?" The cabbie responded, "About $25." When I asked if we could make the 2:51 flight he said, "No problem."

During the ride to Newark, two questions nagged at me. If the flight was full, would I get a seat and would someone else be bumped? Second, what if "no problem" became "a problem" and I missed the flight? Well, the cabbie was right—we made it with time to spare. Oh, yes, the fare! Well, it was $25 on the first meter plus $5 each way for the tunnel plus $6.50 on the second meter, for a total of $41.50!

Conditions at the old Continental terminal in Newark did not surprise me. I knew it would be a zoo, but I was felling pretty good. At least the cabbie went to the right terminal (at that time Continental had absorbed Peoples Express and was operating out of multiple terminals in Newark). I bypassed the long lines and went to the posted gate since the fare for my return ticket out of New York was higher than that of Continental. There was a mob scene at the gate because a few flights had backed up and were departing from the same gate. There was no line—just a mass of bodies. At the check-in desk were two trainees who were mesmerized by the CRT terminal, plus two supervisors processing the passengers while trying to teach the trainees at the same time.

At last it was my turn. I handed the agent my USAir ticket and said I had a reservation on Flight 781 to Cleveland. Notwithstanding the fact that my name was on the ticket, he asked, "Name? You wanna spell it?" I did. He punched the keys on the CRT and scanned the screen, looked up and said, "You had a reservation?"

"Yes," I replied, "On Flight 781 to Cleveland."

"I don't see it. Who made it, your travel agent?"

People behind me and to my left and right were edging closer. I froze, thinking, "Do I dare answer the question?" I mean, this is New York/Newark, the Continental terminal. He is not going to believe me. The other passengers became restless, and the agent grew more impatient. I blurted out, "It was made about 45 minutes ago by a secretary in Manhattan." The agent looked up from the CRT and asked, "What? Who?" I knew better, but couldn't stop myself. "It was made by Mr. Lorenzo's secretary!" With that, the agent looked up and smiled, and then in a loud voice said, "Okay, we got another one, another friend of Frank Lorenzo here with no reservation—the fifth one today!"

Unable to crawl away and hide, I asked if there were any seats on Flight 781 to Cleveland. The agent said he'd put me in coach since it should be available. He then asked to hold my ticket, saying he'd call me back. Without further thought I quickly got lost in the crowd, heading for a phone to call my wife. I wanted her to know I'd changed flights and, if all went well, would be home for dinner. As I hung up, I heard my name being paged to report to the desk at Gate 53.

Wedging my way through the crowd toward the gate, I searched frantically for the phone message containing Frank Lorenzo's New York office number. I was certain it would be needed, strongly suspecting I was about to meet some unfriendly faces from airport security. After all, I'd been the fifth one.

Odd thoughts ran through my mind. "Should I run?" "Will they allow me a phone call?" "Will my next stop be Bellevue?" By that time I had been propelled to the front of the line. There was the same agent, grinning self-consciously. The trainees were standing at attention. I put my hands out for the cuffs but he merely said, "Here is your boarding pass, Mr. Nykiel. Your reservation just came through from New York. Please have a pleasant trip."

As the plane taxied out to the runway, I reflected on the day's events. Had I too, become a cynical consumer? I realized that I had had nothing but negative thoughts about how things would turn out all day. Even at that moment I was wondering if there would be a delay due to mechanical difficulties or weather conditions, why I had left my umbrella in the car, or whether my car would still be where I had left it.

I even began to conjecture about the problems I might have if I had to check into a hotel. Would my reservation be honored? I realized then that I *had* become another victim in the "age of cynicism." And, who was to blame for it? And what could be done to overcome this attitude? If given the opportunity, could (or would) I, the consumer, change?

CONDITIONING OF THE CONSUMER

Many more questions came to mind as the evening progressed. The 6:00 P.M. local news was full of the usual negative local events—layoffs, strikes, crime and its victims, a sex scandal in government, a senator's office staffer taking payoffs. The 7:00 P.M. national news continued with more of the same, the only difference being the slicker dramatizations. It continued the next morning in page after page of the newspapers. There was no escape from the negative barrage and the resulting cynicism.

As I left for work that morning in my son's new car, I again realized there were still more reasons for this conditioning. The car had only 100 miles on it when the exhaust pipe fell off, due to a defective rubber hanger. Upon arrival for the 8:00 A.M. appointment with the dealer's service manager, I received more conditioning. He said, "Gee, wish I could help, but that's a new car and we don't have that part yet. We'll have to order it from the factory—may take a month or so." I'll skip my response, his response, and the interim solution. The point is that, whether the problem is mechanical, social or political, we the consumers have been conditioned to expect the outcome to be negative.

When did it all begin and how did it progress so rapidly? Did it start during the Vietnam era or with the first auto recall—or with the Nixon resignation and Watergate? But when is not really important; nor is the reinforcement by the Chappaquiddick incident, the now infamous "monkey-business" episode involving a Colorado senator, the TV ministry scandal or latest Wall Street fraud or IRS investigation. What is important is that we recognize these occurrences are now being reported so extensively (yes, by the media) that it is virtually all the consumer sees, hears, reads about, and, unfortunately, is now conditioned to expect. So why even expect "good service?" Why should we expect good quality in our products, especially when even new products are defective? Why should consumers believe anyone's product or service promises when they can't even believe their senator, governor, mayor, or TV minister?

And what about service employees? Why should they smile and try to do a good job when the customer has been conditioned to view their efforts with skepticism—especially when their supervisors are more concerned with such things as cost control, pricing, and computer systems?

What has this conditioning done to management's perspective? Has it also succumbed to cynicism? Has cynicism in the marketplace resulted in entrenchment and complacency by management?

THE PROJECT VS. PEOPLE MENTALITY

Some would answer these questions with a loud, "Hell, no!" Others would say "there is a problem." Still others don't even recognize that a problem exists. Why is the captain often the last to know that someone is trying to blow a hole in his ship with a missile that's already been launched? Why do company chairmen find themselves walking the plank because board members have failed to support their plans for a new company name and acquisitions strategy? Has management foregone closeness to the troops in favor of palace strategies? Has the consumer been taken for granted?

Think about management's time, energy, capital, and resources that are focused on such things as a new name for the company, leather seats in first class, color selection; atrium designs, or menus and decor. The mentality seems to be, "If you build it bigger, better or brighter, and promote it with large ad dollars, motivational sales tactics, and gimmicks, you are on target and will succeed." Perhaps one of the best examples of this project vs. people mentality comes from the hotel industry.

Today there are an abundance of spectacular hotels, complete with atriums, gourmet dining, and extensive meeting and health club facilities. But the odds on finding a warm, friendly, efficient, and competent staff in one of these spectacular hotels, are about the same as making a tight connection at O'Hare.

Why? Well, one reason is that management is defining excellence in terms of concrete—not the needs of the consumer. I know of one hotel chain which, over four years ago, held extensive, expensive, and frequent meetings to discuss such things as amenities, cost containment, development, exercise facilities, food and beverage, garage policies, carpets, curtains, computers, and floor tiles; yet, not one meeting focused on personal customer service such as guest contact points and expectations, and empathy training.

They were not alone. Other companies in service-related industries will spend millions on new computer systems, but not dime number one on finding out what the consumer thinks and wants—or doesn't want.

The project vs. people mentality is understandable in a society that values the spectacular, size, and unit growth. This mentality is even easier to understand in such sectors of the service industry as airlines, banks, hotels, and hospitals, where concern for the consumer (or patient) is not a rung to the top of the management ladder. That is not to say there are no firms that recognize the need for a balance between consumer expectations and product/service fulfillment. Nor is this to say that one should rise to the top solely through consumer market research. What could be more important to the company than how consumers think, and what will produce positive (or negative) responses?

One vivid example involved passenger van colors for an upscale hotel chain. Over a two-year period, the chain spent hundreds of thousands of dollars on developing a new image as well as new vans for its guests. The vans were painted a rich silver/gray with gold and maroon lettering and accents to match the color in its advertising, uniforms, and decor. One day, a particular hotel manager and his appointed designer announced to a senior management that their new van had arrived for all to see. And there it stood—painted green! In fact, the designer had ordered the same green with the same yellow accents used by one of the country's largest (and then aging) motel chains. Had the designer or general manager even considered the confusion this would create for their customers? What was the tired and harried traveler to look for—the expected silver/gray van of the upscale chain or the new, green, motel look-alike? The designer protested, "We wanted to try a rich green." The general manager's response was that it had a new seat configuration and that the British green was an "in" color. How was the consumer waiting at the local airport to know that this green van, which was different from all the others of the chain at all the other airports, belonged to that hotel?

Elementary though this example may be, it is frequently repeated in the service industry. Banks are not open when people need them, insurance companies' policies require interpretation by attorneys, credit card companies provide "customer service" toll-free numbers answered by recordings, hospitals process human beings like cattle, and retail stores run sales but neglect to provide enough cashiers or salespersons.

Simply stated, management's focus has not been on the customer. It has been on systems, processing, controls, outlets, work flow, and, yes, project vs. people mentality. Just as the cashier diligently enters inventory control codes, the consumer grows more cynical of the retailer's ability to service quickly—and in this case—actually take payment! And just as one bank eliminates evening hours, the consumer rightfully voices his disapproval by moving his accounts across the street or to another town in search of someone who'll understand his need to bank in the evening.

Hey, wait a minute, you may say. What about such things as automated teller machines, 24-hour banking, and magnetic tape credit card readers? Aren't these an indication that management is responding? What about those good old motivators—like competitive pricing, sales, and discounts—that make it worthwhile to wait in line? In answer I say that additional questions must be asked: What is the level of consumer satisfaction? How are services being rated?

Are consumers happy about their travel experiences? What is the general mood of the marketplace?

Pendulums and Perspectives

Two main keys to formulating management strategy involve analyzing the direction in which the pendulum is swinging, and then anticipating how far it will go, and for how long. It is evident that the cynical environment that has been developing for 20-plus years may, one day in a utopian society, become non-existent. In all likelihood, however, there are enough problems to ensure its continuance for another 20 years. What does this mean for those in the service industries? It means that the consumer will make choices based on competitive offerings. It means that there will be winners—those who understand and respond to the changing perspective of consumers and provide frontline consumer-contact employees with training, strategies, and motivational techniques. It means there will be losers—those whose project vs. people mentality perspective precludes them from meeting the consumer's expectations.

II

Ten Steps to Service Success

A few weeks prior to the trip to New York previously mentioned, I had read *Moments of Truth*, by Jan Carlson, President, SAS. Reflecting on the examples of the airline's service success described, I considered the major lessons that could be learned.

Two thoughts came to mind in relation to my New York experience with the airline reservationists. First, the recognition of the critical points of contact in relationships with customers. These weren't really "moments of truth" as much as they were *"points of encounter"*—opportunities to relate in a positive manner to the customer's expectations. Second, what appeared to be wrong with the services I'd experienced (and with service firms in general). No one seemed to be aware of those key *points of encounter*; no one recognized the opportunity to win my loyalty and overcome my cynicism. Well, what should I have expected from a project vs. people mentality or a hi-tech mentality? Points of encounter with people are not their main focus; a CRT terminal *was* the focal point!

RECOGNITION OF THE *POINTS OF ENCOUNTER*

The points at which your employees encounter the consumer are opportunities to win (or lose) the consumer.

In the age of cynicism in America, we must take the first step toward achieving service success: recognition. This is not the obvious recognition after the fact that service problems have caused sales to slip or that another company has taken more market share. Such problem recognition is reactive rather than proactive. For recognition to be proactive, observation and analysis of the *points of encounter* must occur. Quite simply this means we must focus on the interaction of our product or service with the consumer.

How often had you heard, "They really have a problem here. Too bad they haven't recognized and fixed it." "They" usually refers to top management, which has skipped the all-important thought process known as "recognition." A decline in sales, employee turnover, consumer complaints—these are all "reactive" indicators.

True recognition in the proactive sense means knowing the *points of encounter* and studying them on an ongoing basis. Yet it is amazing how many firms have made it virtually impossible for their management to be in a position to recognize the *points of encounter*. In essence, by blinding itself to the reality of the marketplace, management has prohibited proactive recognition.

An appropriate image of the project vs. people mentality is management blinding itself in mirrored glass in its limousines. Picture the hotel executive being met at the airport and whisked off in the hotel's limo, bypassing his own vans and cabs—his hotel's first *point of encounter*. He then bypasses the front desk encounter by being taken to his room by a member of the hotel's management team. I could go on to describe the prompt room service and the superb gourmet meal, all the way to bypassing the infamous check-out counter—another important *point of encounter* that is missed.

A STEP UP AND A STEP DOWN

I changed jobs, leaving a "motel" chain to work for a luxury hotel chain. Because motels are smaller and less complicated to operate, the owner or manager can actually expedite check-in of the smaller number of customers, whereas in the larger luxury hotels, this job is relegated to an hourly wage employee. Frequently the line of people awaiting check-in can be five deep!

When I joined this luxury chain, my first observation was the problem at the front desk: the room clerks were being hassled as the result of the 6:00 P.M. check-in rush. I saw this in a half-dozen of our large hotels during my orientation visits.

One day I was asked to tell the president (my boss) my reactions to what I had observed. Before I could begin, he said, "Quite a difference from those no-frills motels—more top-flight services, great food, and a real quality feel." I replied, "We do have some magnificent buildings, some excellent food, but a few service problems." This last statement really upset him. He asked, "What do you mean, service problems?" "Well, for one thing," I responded, "the airport vans are hard to find because they all have different colors and bear individual hotel names rather than our chain's name. I'm not sure how a new customer can know what to look for. Second, check-in and check-out are pretty bad—there are long lines and no management personnel available." My boss thought for a minute and then said, "I'll have to look into that—which hotel?" "All of the hotels I visited," I replied. It was obvious we were about to have a "communications" problem (that's what presidents call it when subordinates don't share their point of view). Then it dawned on me that every time I had met my boss prior to this meeting, he'd arrived by limousine from the airport, personally escorted by a management person directly to his room. How could he have recognized the problem? He always bypassed the *points of encounter*! Needless to say, that chain now has clearly identifiable airport vans (in limousine condition), and a very good express check-in and check-out service.

In order to recognize whether or not your firm has a problem with service, you must frequently put yourself in the role of the ordinary customer. It will do miracles for your powers of recognition, even though it may raise your blood pressure in the process.

STEP II

IDENTIFICATION OF PROBLEMS

Recognition of *points of encounter* and service problems is but one proactive step to service success. I say proactive because, in the case just described, the boss did go out as a consumer, did see the problem, and did take action, all before major harm had been done.

What is this process by which one can assure preemptive recognition and prevent loss of market share or customers? Although there are a number of approaches, placing yourself in the role of customer is one of the best. Ideally it should be done incognito and often. It will make you aware of a service problem or at least give you a fresh look at the customer's perspective. While I shall suggest some periodic acid tests (likely to give you acid indigestion), try to be observant and analytical. Always record the problems and think about possible solutions. If you can't control yourself and blow your cover, show the employees the correct way; don't just reprimand or berate them. But I'm getting ahead of myself. Here are some procedures to follow:

- Call the toll-free number of one of your service establishments and analyze the response.

- Go incognito to your outlets, service centers, ticket counters, or check-in desks and make notes of your observations (you may need a big notepad). Ask other customers about their experiences at the *points of encounter.*

- Go to one of your sales offices and read your literature (after all, your name or signature is likely to be on it).

- Observe your staff. Are they empathetic with your customers?

- After making these observations, go through the entire purchasing process and/or service experience and make a list of the direct *points of encounter.*

Review this list with the following objectives:

1. Identification of the critical points at which the sale, loyalty or purchase can be lost instantly if not handled properly.

2. Identification of the points that have to be corrected.

3. Identification of the points that present opportunities for making your service stand out above the competition.

Year after year Delta Airlines is rated highly for its service. As a frequent traveler, I've observed that Delta's aircraft are no different from other airlines (in fact, some are not as plush). The terminal is no different and the food is not better. Why the high rating?

Because Delta, knowingly or unknowingly, is performing very well at some key *points of encounter*. The people in reservations show confidence and have a helpful attitude. The check-in employees are relatively efficient; the red coats worn by gate personnel stand out, and they give the impression of being available to direct passengers to where they have to go.

Some call this efficiency. Some say it is just performing the basics correctly. It certainly does not reflect a project vs. people mentality attitude. Quite simply, it is a matter of relating to customers and executing well at the *points of encounter*. That bright, red blazer and smiling face mean a lot to a harried or first-time traveler, especially at a busy hub airport.

For years a number of hotel chains have offered a complimentary newspaper as a customer service. In doing so, they have identified a *point of encounter*, where they can make the guest "feel at home." However, a few hotel companies have recognized a real opportunity to "stand out." At Stouffer Hotels and Resorts a guest gets more than a newspaper haphazardly tossed at the door. A highly visible card in the room says, "Complimentary coffee and newspaper with wake-up call." And when guests call in the evening to request a wake-up call, the operator asks them what morning beverage they prefer. Within a few minutes after receiving that wake-up call, the beverage with china cup and stainless-steel pot, and newspaper arrive on a lined tray—delivered by a smiling employee.

Stouffer not only recognized the service need, more importantly, they identified the key service concepts. This is a proactive strategy to win the customer's loyalty. I myself have become so accustomed to the wake-up service at Stouffer that I miss it when I stay at hotels where it is not offered, where the paper is merely tossed by the door, or where nothing at all is provided.

One word of caution. When you recognize a *point of encounter*, identify an opportunity, and offer a service, be sure that it is done well. It "ain't only what you do, but the way that you do it."

Recognition and Identification Tips

1.   Use a shoppers' service to check on your business.*

2.   Conduct your own service audit.

3.   Talk to and, more importantly, listen to your customers.

4.   Observe and experience the offerings of your most successful competitors.

* Even if you are hesitant about utilizing shoppers' services or believe your internal checking system is adequate, use one at least periodically. Recently I observed a quality control check being conducted at a local McDonald's—the same one that features their famous "touch pad cash registers." At this particular unit the key pads were so worn that, in the previous six visits I had been charged for only partial orders (sometimes less than half the actual cost). I certainly hope McDonald's has a shoppers' service checking on their hassled personnel with those "consumer friendly" registers. If not, my guess is they could be losing millions of dollars a day. So, at a minimum, a shopper's service will tell you if you are charging correctly.

5. Experience your own service *as a customer*.

6. Personally review a random sample of complaint letters once per quarter.

7. Solicit the opinions of your service offering from a focus research group every few years.

8. List all *"points of encounter"* and have your management focus on one of these points each quarter.

9. Check current relevance of all points of encounter training material and procedures. Update where appropriate.

10. Spend at least as much time on the *points of encounter* as you do on the project aspects of your business.

PLANS OF ACTION

Having made your observations incognito, prepared lists, identified *points of encounter*, and come up with several ideas to combat consumer cynicism, you now need a plan of action. Before implementing it on a wide scale, test it to make sure it is executed properly. Not to do so can be disastrous. For example, at Stouffer, they don't shoot from the hip. They didn't just declare that newspapers and wake-up calls were to be provided at all their hotels.

First, they selected a test hotel and wrote an operation/execution plan. Guess what? It didn't work! The plan called for the food and beverage department to treat the coffee and newspaper delivery as if it were room service—just run it up from the kitchen after the wake-up calls were completed. As a result, calls and service were sometimes as much as 60 minutes apart. A new plan had prepared trays placed on a cart in the service areas on each floor. In addition, depending on the hotel's floor plan, phone lists were preprinted with wake-up call by room number. In short, the rooms department, utilizing early-morning personnel, took over execution from food and beverage. Can you imagine the chaos if Stouffer hadn't tested before going chainwide? Today, the plan is in written form, and is part of the training program and the employee's performance evaluation.

SOLVING SOME PROBLEM IS NO SOLUTION

The best-laid plans should not only be tested, but evaluated periodically. For example, another large chain recognized that the complaint calls about lack of cleanliness they received tied up the order-taking switchboards. A quick solution was sought, and came in the form of readily available comment card. Then came the CEO's even brighter idea. Instead of the comment (complaint) being sent to headquarters, they should go directly to the unit managers so that they could take immediate action. The cards were then to be batched and sent to headquarters monthly. They even made a reduction in complaints a bonus-criterion! In addition, the CEO (strongly supported by the CFO) noted the postage that would be saved. To them this was a double-win solution. Win number one—a release mechanism for customer complaints with less hassle that was quickly actionable; and win number two—it was accomplished at less cost. Unfortunately this "win-win" turned into a loser!

During the first meeting following installation of the comment card program, the CEO complimented a few of the unit managers for having the least number of complaints about cleanliness. He also warned a few for still having a large number of complaint cards. At cocktails that evening one of those praised was asked how he did it. "You sit in the middle of filth, your unit was damn near shut down by the health department, yet your complaint factor was one of the lowest?" His answer was, "I'm the one who mails in the cards, but I screen them first. Why cut off your own legs?"

Months later the comment card system was abruptly discontinued when the number one-ranked unit for least complaints was shut down by the health department!

The damage had been done. More and more units were losing volume, being cited for cleanliness violations, and company-wide cutbacks were in progress. In this case, the mistake was obvious; however, "fixing" the problems can be complex and requires a plan of action that is thoroughly thought out.

REALLOCATION OF RESOURCES

Recognition, identification, and a plan of action are sometimes not enough to make the necessary change at a *point of encounter*. To remain competitive and successful, a reallocation of resources sometimes may be required.

These resources may be financial, personnel or equipment. As a Hertz Platinum Card service holder, I am amazed at how well this VIP service works. And, for a while I was amazed that Hertz offered this service to so few people. I thought, with fewer than 5,000 members and the costs involved, it must be a loser.

For those of you who are unfamiliar with the Hertz Platinum Card, here is how it works: On personal approval by Hertz's chairman, the card is issued to executives such as chairmen, CEOs, presidents, and selected VIP "decision-makers." The service provides a separate ID card, a separate computer program; separate color-coordinated and designed collateral materials; a comprehensive staff training program; and a separate toll-free number.

How can Hertz make money on only a few thousand cards issued? Why would they allocate all these resources for such a small group? Why would Hertz have an employee meet you at the airport, allow you to by-pass the lines, the bus, just *give* you the keys to the car—at the curb—and let you go? Why would they tell you that if you don't have time to return the car to the Hertz drop-off, you can just leave it where it is and they'll pick it up? Why?

Because Hertz is in the service business, and recognizes the "limousine" principle of "influence." Just as a casino provides a private jet, limousine or suite for a high roller, Hertz provides VIP service for the decision-makers—those people who ultimately decide which car rental company will be used by their firm. In this case, Hertz recognized and identified a *point of encounter* and the opportunity to distinguish itself and, in spite of the short-term "not profitable" outlook for such a service, reallocated financial resources, personnel, and equipment to support the plan. The net result is likely to be millions of dollars in rentals and fleet leases from the companies whose ultimate decision-makers have been "personally" invited to benefit from the Platinum Service.

Not every reallocation step may be as slick as Platinum Service. Some, while less pleasing to the ego, also contribute to service success.

Simple reallocations, such as putting on more phone operators to eliminate the interminable rings followed by a recorded voice telling you all lines or service representatives are busy, can set your company ahead of the competition. I would guess that half the callers hang up before the "next available service representative" comes on the line—that is, if they haven't been disconnected or forgotten who they'd called in the first place!

If a firm never puts you on "hold" or has your call

answered by a recording; if you are always connected with a professional service representative, the chances of your becoming and remaining its customer are pretty good.

STEP V

PRIORITIZATION
OF EXECUTION

The step least often taken and most often needed is prioritization. In a recent edition of the Sunday *New York Times* I came across two very interesting help-wanted ads that may serve as examples. One fairly large block ad from Beth Israel Medical center in New York sought a "Director of Guest Relations" (new position). The other from a nationally recognized medical clinic read, "Wanted—Complaints Clerk." To me it was obvious that Beth Israel had (1) recognized that it was in a service business; (2) identified a *point of encounter* opportunity; (3) established a plan of action; (4) reallocated resources; and (5) prioritized the importance of relationship with its patients. Note the difference in perspectives. Beth Israel views its patients as "guests," and the person who relates to them is at a director's level. These are the obvious signs of a healthy proactive service perspective. On the other hand, the medical clinic has the classical reactive mentality of looking for a "complaints" person and prioritizes this function with the label of "clerk." Which medical facility do you think will be perceived as better able to provide service?

Today, hospitals, insurance companies, financial

institutions, and retailers are all in a highly competitive marketplace that demands prioritization and frequent adjustments. While the following is also a medical community example, it will demonstrate what happens when the need for prioritization is perceived but is executed as mere window dressing.

At one of this nation's more renowned "clinics" this is the patient relations process: After each appointment, a comment card is mailed to the patient with a message from the "Chairman of the Board" and a brief questionnaire with one line for "additional comments." Now, while this might signal a very positive approach, this is how it actually works, based upon a recent personal experience.

A SYSTEM GONE
HAYWIRE

I had returned from a business trip and found that my wife had severe pains in her shoulder, neck, and right arm. Since it was Saturday afternoon, I knew that I would have to go to the emergency room of a clinic. After the usual lengthy wait (1½ to 2 hours) a young resident who had difficulty speaking English examined my wife. As he was doing so, she explained that she had some spinal/back problems and when they occurred she was usually treated in the orthopedic department; however, since the pain was severe, she had come to the emergency room. After a brief examination, the young doctor said, "It could be the back, a disc, or nerve pinch, or it could be some badly pulled muscles, or it could be shingles." I said, "What?" The young doctor elaborated on "shingles" for about ten minutes (he must have just completed a dissertation on the subject). He then said, "I'd like you to see your back doctor here at the clinic on Monday. I'll note that on your records. You should call for an appointment. Now, if you get worse before then, just call here. It could be shingles."

On Monday my wife called the clinic for an appointment with the orthopedic doctor. The person who took the call promised to get back to her after the doctor had evaluated the resident's report.

When I returned home from work that evening, there in the mail was that "Chairman-of-the-Board" message and questionnaire. I wrote the following letter after my wife had received treatment from a different medical group for some badly pulled muscles and pinched nerves. (In the interim, still another questionnaire arrived from the clinic.)

Dear Chairman of the Board:
Re: Clinic No. 476–018–965–44139–1
Thank you for your message and questionnaires. I apologize for not using the one line (referenced comments) at the bottom of the form, but you did say to write if there were any problems. I know you're busy so I'll be brief.
On May 18 (one month ago today) my wife called to make an appointment in the orthopedic department. She did this per instructions by the resident (your shingles expert) in the emergency room. We called four times and each time were told that someone

would call us back to set up an appointment—that Dr. B just had to review the resident's report and patient history. However, the appointment desk had not yet received his instructions. So, after the four calls, the passage of four weeks, and no return call from the appointment desk, can you tell me if Dr. B is on sabbatical?

As a businessman, I see how competitive the medical marketplace has become in our community. I personally desire the "best" for my wife; that's why we chose your reputedly outstanding clinic. However, if I treated my valued customers in the way your appointment deskperson and Dr. B treated us, I'm sure they would no longer be my customers. We'd still like to be yours. May we hear from someone? (but please, not the shingles expert). Thank you.

Sincerely,
Dr. Ronald A. Nykiel

P.S. My home phone is . . . .
My office phone is . . . .
My home address is . . . .
My office address is . . . .

Several weeks passed before I received a phone call at the office from someone who called himself an "ombudsman." Webster's Dictionary defines ombudsman as "1. A government official as in Sweden or New Zealand appointed to receive or investigate complaints made by individuals against abuses or capricious acts of public officials. 2. One that investigates reported complaints (as from students or consumers), reports findings, and helps to achieve equitable settlements."

Thus, an ombudsman is a "go-between," a problem-solver, a referee of sorts. Obviously I expected an apology for what must have been a mix-up. What I heard instead was incredible.

"Mr. Nykiel, thank you for calling—oops—I'm sorry, I called you—these phones—anyways, I just wanted to know if the appointment desk was polite when they called you to make the appointment. Was it satisfactory?"

I said, "Are you calling about my letter to the chairman of the board?"

The young woman replied, "Yes, hasn't your wife been seen yet?"

"No."

"Oh, I see. When is her appointment?"

"No one has called me back to set one up."

"Oh, well, let me check into it. I'll get back to you. . . ."

So here is a magnificent clinic, with an appropriate message and questionnaire system in place—even an ombudsman—still unable to set up an appointment after more than four weeks. Where is prioritization in all this?

My guess is that the focus is just not on the patient (customer). During that four-week period, construction of another new building was announced, another new satellite clinic proposed, and a research project breakthrough publicized (no, it wasn't on shingles). Again, we have the concentration on projects rather than people. Yes, the proper steps—recognition, identification, plan of action; even reallocation of (some) resources had been taken, but everyone from the chairman of the board down to the appointment desk clerk, all seem to have forgotten the basic function of a medical facility—to help patients get well!

Reallocation and Prioritization Tips

1. In order of priority, list the *points of encounter* that need new or additional resources.

2. In order of priority, list all "projects" (capital) dollars scheduled for allocation.

3. Now prepare a new list which in order of priority blends the *points of encounter* items and "projects" items together.

4. In identifying your "projects" capital needs, first prioritize those that relate to your *points of encounter*.

5. Review your *non-point of encounter* personnel count and payroll costs.

6. Review your *point of encounter* personnel count and payroll costs.

7. Allocate your resources to address the *point of encounter* personnel and related costs to do their job right on a top priority basis. Can you imagine a firm that would spend a half-million dollars on a project and deny *point of encounter* employees an increase of 50 cents per hour incentive pay or a

$5,000 training program? Review all of your firm's expenses; this could be called "current shock."

If prioritization were a fully executed step as in the clinic example, behavior by the chairman's office all the way down to the appointment clerk would have been different. What appears to be missing in many of today's service-sector operations is trained personnel. It was obvious to me that, had a number of people been trained, the response to me—the customer— would have been timely and, moreover, accurate. Even today many firms recognize the importance of customer relations, yet fail to act at the points of encounter.

A TALE OF TWO SERVICES

Recently, I purchased a new Pontiac for my son. In addition to the high ratings it received from *Consumer Reports and Motor Trend*, I was impressed with the sincerity of the seasoned sales manager at what I'll refer to as Frank's Pontiac. I was even more impressed a week or so later when I received a personal letter from the sales manager inviting me to give him a call if any adjustments or service were required on the car. But a few days later another letter arrived from the service manager welcoming me to the Frank's family of well-maintained and professionally serviced autos. The letter said, "Just call me if I can be of help." As fate would have it, the very next Saturday when my son came home from college, he showed me a dragging tailpipe, barely attached by a split rubberlike hanger.

After blaming Junior for the problem, and finding that Frank's was closed, we went to the local Midas Muffler shop for help. At 5:45 P.M. on a Saturday afternoon, the shop manager at Midas takes the time to look at the problem. He checks on the part and says it is not in inventory but offers to try to fix it so the car can be driven until the part comes in. He suggests it be taken back to the Pontiac dealer, agreeing that it is ridiculous for this to happen with a new car.

The manager spent about five minutes modifying another rubber hanger and then installed it. I was deeply grateful that he had taken care of us late on a Saturday afternoon and even more so that he had been so creative in solving the problem. When I asked how much I owed him, he said, "No charge, you shouldn't have to pay to have a brand-new car fixed. Just come back and see me when you need one of our services."

The following Monday I called Frank's and asked for the sales manager. Unfortunately, he was off on Mondays, so I asked for the service manager (who didn't work on Saturday or Sunday). I was actually quickly connected to service and greeted pleasantly. I explained that the new Pontiac with approximately 100 miles on the odometer had a dragging tailpipe and muffler caused by a split rubber hanger, and asked for an 8:00 A.M. appointment on Thursday morning. The response was, "No problem—we'll see you at 8:00 on Thursday."

My son followed me to the shop and I pulled in behind several other Frank's loyalists. After about ten minutes my turn came. I gave my name and said that I had an 8:00 appointment. The employee looked at me and said, "We don't make appointments. It's first-come, first-served, but you're O.K. for today. What's the problem?" I said, "You can see from this split hanger that it must have been defective when installed." He replied, "Yeah, someone must have over-tightened and split it at the factory. Hell, you have only 150 miles on this car. What's holding the tailpipe up?" I told him that in order to be able to get the car to the dealership, the Midas shop had affixed the tailpipe by modifying a similar part from a Chrysler inventory of rubber hangers. He said, "We'll have it for you by 5:00 P.M. Just sign here."

After work, my son and I drove back to the dealer to pick up the car. The cashier said, "No charge—your car is out back in the lot." I looked at the bill. It read, "Part needs to be ordered from factory—inventory out." Just then I saw the man who had taken the car and I asked him what the bill meant. He replied, "We've had a few cars with this problem and we're all out of rubber hangers right now. We'll call you as soon as they come in." By this time my son had returned. He said, "Dad, I can't drive the car, the tailpipe and muffler are touching the ground." Of course, a lengthy discussion followed such comments as, "I haven't paid for that new car yet," to "How in the hell do you expect me to drive it for six weeks?" Finally, the employee located the hanger Midas had supplied and put it back on the car.

By then I was pretty angry and asked to speak to Mr. Black, the service manager. The employee replied, "Mr. Black hasn't worked here for months." "Well, how come I got this letter from him last week?" The employee glanced at my letter and said, "Oh, are they still sending those out?" And walked away.

Obviously, Frank's Pontiac had reinforced my cynicism about automobile dealer service; their employees had received no training in handling customers. Even the letter that was mailed automatically to new car owners had the name of an employee who was no longer with the company.

Previously, I had read Midas's ads with skepticism, especially when they claimed they would remain open until a problem was solved. This cynical consumer hardly expected to actually receive the service advertised. Midas Muffler obviously recognizes, identifies, plans action, reallocates resources, prioritizes, and trains their personnel very well.

I would be remiss if I didn't say that my previously mentioned experiences with the Hertz Platinum car service was among the best I've ever had, including their training program. Hertz is also one of the best I've encountered. So, so long, Frank's Pontiac—and hats off to Midas and Hertz!

RECRUITING THE RIGHT PERSONNEL

An old "Montanaism" (at least that's where the guy was from who frequently said this) is that "you can't teach a pig to dance." You have to know the right recruiting questions to ask: What are the criteria for those who will be *point-of-encounter* employees? Do any of these employees sell, quote prices, or directly interface with the potential customer at the critical *point of encounter*—the actual purchase of your service? If so, what type of employee do you want to be responsible for bringing in revenue? Are these employees trainable; are they sufficiently intelligent to hold such positions or are they *overqualified*? If you can't answer most of these questions readily, your firm is either already in trouble or will be in trouble before very long.

Well thought out recruiting criteria can provide very great rewards, and should be reviewed frequently. When did you last re-evaluate job descriptions and hiring criteria for such positions as cashier, reservations agent, teller, flight attendant, rental agent, admissions clerk, sales representative, and agent? Have you been hiring "pigs" and expecting them to dance?

If you believe there is no need for such reviews because the service you offer has not changed, you are very wrong; your consumer is changing constantly.

Some advocate turning the organization chart upside down, while others suggest that the pay scales be reversed. Obviously, there is no simple answer for all service-industry firms. All the steps must be taken into account: recognition, identification, plan of action, reallocation, prioritization, training, and recruiting.

Recruiting should be attempted only after a complete review of each *point-of-encounter* position. Complexity of job function as well as the types of consumers encountered on a daily basis should be thoroughly analyzed. Do you have (or want) minimum-wage clerks directly interfacing with $100,000-plus executives?

Consider the wages paid to managers whose primary jobs may be working with intangibles or filling out forms, then look at those employees who relate directly to the consumer. Can those who are closest to the *points of encounter* "learn to dance?" I am always amazed that firms willing to invest $50 million in a hotel will not pay 50 cents an hour more for front desk personnel; that airlines are content to spend millions on aircraft, fancy lounges, and uniforms, while shaving a few thousand on counter agents and phone lines.

Recently I conducted a panel discussion of consumers whose profile included some with yearly incomes in excess of $100,000. They traveled extensively (15 or more trips a year). We had been discussing the hassles of travel for some time when I asked each for a summary statement. One top executive from the

Geneva Corporation said, "I guess when you pay first-class rates, the least you can expect is that someone welcome you with a smile." There was instant agreement by the other panelists who felt that a simple smile is about all it would take to change their perception of the service they received. The well-traveled probably have more reasons than most to be cynical. Ironically, I've often seen senior executives in the service industry veto "empathy" training for *point-of-encounter* employees, calling this type of training "B.S." Why is this happening in today's service industry? One reason is that we need to change recruitment criteria for managers and executives in order to include some consumer orientation.

Throughout the service industry we find examples of traditional (or perhaps the word is "antiquated") recruiting criteria. Insurance firms look for agents with "computer familiarity" rather than "consumer familiarity." Restaurant managers graduate from college with a degree in "hospitality" but have no expertise in consumer relations. Tellers and cashiers are often recruited solely on their proficiency in mathematics. Hell, after a good meal you don't want to interface with an auditor!

As a consumer, I am always pleased when I stop at a Friendly's restaurant or stay at a Marriott. The people are always outgoing and consistently provide a high level of service. The waitresses and waiters are hustling *and* smiling. The desk clerks, bellmen, and other *point-of-encounter* personnel always seem to have a positive attitude and enthusiasm for their jobs. I am convinced that both of these organizations seek out *point-of-encounter* employees who are outgoing and trainable.

Training and Recruiting Tips for the Boss

1. Have members of top management participate in at least one *point-of-encounter* position training session.

2. Have members of top management work at least one eight-hour day (preferably an entire week) in one of the *point-of-encounter* positions.

3. Review your training resources (people, procedures and related budgets) annually to determine if they are adequate in preparing your personnel for service leadership.

4. Ask customers to evaluate (via questionnaire or direct contact) how well they believe *point-of-encounter* employees are trained.

5. Ask newly trained employees what else they believe should be taught.

6. Ask the same question of your seasoned employees.

7. Instruct all recruiters of *point-of-encounter* employees to ask themselves whether they would want to deal face-to-face with the person they are considering for the job.

8. Personally participate in at least one interview session for a *point-of-encounter* employee.

9. Consider upgrading your pay scale to attract seasoned pros away from the competition.

10. Make sure your recruiters know exactly what you expect of them and then, periodically check to see that they are doing exactly what you want.

COMMUNICATIONS

When it comes to communicating with the customer, no one is more important than the *point-of-encounter* employee. It is this employee that is often the first to know when (and if) your service offering, price, policy, or procedural change is working. He or she is also a great source of information when you attempt to improve service.

But when it comes to communicating with these employees, the corporate hierarchy in general, does a terrible job. This, in tandem with the consumer who is cynical, works to create the environment for disastrous service.

There are many examples of good and bad communication in the service industry. A case in point is CEO Bill Marriott, Jr., who is famous for his visits to virtually every hotel, restaurant, or in-flight kitchen in Marriott's multibillion dollar empire. These are not your typical "presidential" appearances, but detailed inspections as well as walk-throughs to instill motivation. Mistakes are pointed out. Employee suggestions are recorded and implemented on a broad scale if they are worthwhile.

Adherence to "Standard Operating Procedures" (SOPs) is mandatory at Marriott. It is therefore no coincidence that Marriott's operations and services are efficient and consistent. There are other examples, but the important point is the same in all situations—good communications. The conscientious CEO goes beyond motivation and inspection. The *point-of-encounter* employees are made aware of top management's interest in seeing not only how the job is being done, but also who is doing the job.

By definition, "communication" connotes a two-way flow—up and down. Small ideas turn into big winners if communication channels are open.

Take the case of the bellman who suggested that baggage carts should have larger air-filled tires rather than the small, harder-rubber and metal ones. This was a simple idea that made the job easier, dramatically reduced noise level in hallways, extended the life of the equipment, reduced downtime due to repairs, the accident rate on carts that tended to tip over, and work-related injuries.

There are obviously many communication "break-downs" in any service business. How often have you encountered a ticket or rental agent, or front desk clerk who looked at you blankly when you asked about one of the company's promotional offers? How often have you gone into a branch of a national service establishment, armed with its own ad, only to have the sales personnel stare at the ad and then shout out, "Do we honor this offer?" Nice reinforcement of the cynical consumer attitude!

For some reason, it is easier to inform one million customers of your offer than one thousand *point-of-encounter* employees. There appears to be one logical explanation. Your ad or service offer goes directly from you to the consumer, but the memo describing that offer is often handed down from the vice president of marketing through the managers to the unit managers to the department managers to the shift managers and, finally to the *point-of-encounter* employees. Plenty of opportunity for a breakdown in communication. It happens all the time.

One thing is sure: Never assume that your detailed memo of instructions, the training video and/or manual have been read, viewed, or understood by those who must use the information. The best way to find out is to put on the consumer's hat and try to get the service you have offered. Don't be surprised at what you find out.

Remember what happened when banks first offered ATMs (automatic teller machines)? First, there was a communications process to convince consumers to use the machine. Then the unexpected occurred. Consumers accepted ATMs as a way of making cash withdrawals, but the "deposit" side of the equation had not been communicated adequately. Psychologically, it was a difficult concept to accept. People had no qualms about punching a few keys and taking $100 in cash, however, very few trusted the machine with deposits. In fact, Society National Bank in Ohio sent its ATM "Green Machine" cardholders a $2-deposit coupon that would be credited to their individual account in an effort to get them to try making a deposit. And this occurred over a year after the ATM was introduced!

Any form of change may be difficult to communicate, and the difficulty can be compounded when the change involves behavior. Machines similar to ATMs (I would call them "automatic *transaction* machines") have been introduced at other locations such as airline terminals, hotels, and car rental agencies. Their acceptance has been far from smashing. One reason is the poor communication job that has been done by the firms who introduced them. The "benefits" to consumers have not been sufficiently touted; therefore consumers have not been motivated to make the needed behavioral change.

Ironically, the situations most frequent travelers complain about are long lines for check-in and checkout. During my last stay at the Los Angeles Airport Hilton, I observed a line 20 deep, waiting to check in. A machine was in place which they could have used, but half of those people just stared at it as though it were an out-of-order video game. The same was true for the Shuttle flights at LaGuardia, although there were a few brave souls trying it. Avis has always been technologically innovative. They now have a "hi-tech no-touch" car check-in process which uses a super hand-held computer-printer. If we take the following Avis example through the steps to service success, we'll see why it is a winner on all counts—especially the communication step.

Avis *recognized* that the frequent traveler dislikes lines when returning a car. Most drove in with little time to spare for making their flight, and many felt they needed to take the rental bill with them rather than use an express drop-off box, because they wanted to be able to file their expense reports and be reimbursed promptly. Next, Avis *identified* that the automated machines for car check-in were not (as per previous reasons cited) gaining acceptance. Avis also identified the components of the check-in return process by literally following it all the way through from the remote return area to the bus and back to the terminal. Further, they sought to determine what technology could be used to lessen the time it took to provide the customer with a final bill.

Using all the findings, the action plan was developed. The *point-of-encounter* was moved back to when the customer first enters the return lot, extending the "return counter" by use of technology—the hand-held computer-printer. When you pull into the lot to return your car, an Avis agent notes your mileage and fuel level (having already entered your license-plate number). The information is simultaneously transmitted by radio to the computer which, in turn, transmits your statement to the hand-held computer-printer within 60 seconds.

The agent was moved into the lot, as close as possible to the first *point of encounter*. By the time you put on your jacket or take your briefcase from the trunk, the agent has your printed statement ready to be clipped to your expense report. This is a win-win process that is well communicated to customer and employee. Most importantly, customers were not asked to modify their behavior.

By moving the agent into the lot and investing in new software, Avis reallocated its resources to improve dramatically its service at a key *point of encounter*. Further, Avis gave this new and unique check-in process top priority. The prioritization extended from operations to marketing to training to advertising to human resources to technical services. The retraining and recruiting focused on enabling agents to record quickly mileage and plate numbers, and acquire the necessary skills for using the computer-printer.

Even more importantly, Avis communicated—first, to its own management regarding the significance of the technological breakthrough, and second, to its *point-of encounter* agents. Third, they communicated through to the consumer clear, illustrated, descriptive advertising, which pointed out the benefits of the system. Moreover, the same advertising clearly demonstrated two other key points: no behavioral change was required of the customers, and they would not have to stand in line to receive their bills. Thus, the communications message resulted in two wins for the customer: (1) No hassle (less time/no line); (2) a printed bill on the spot.

STEP IX

FOLLOW-UP TO EXECUTION

Let's go back to Bill Marriott with regard to communications. All those walk-throughs would not have amounted to much unless there had been a positive form of follow-up. In the process either a note was sent to the unit in question reaffirming the action to be taken or for the subject to be discussed upon the next visit. Granted, the man has a phenomenal memory, but the key point is that because there is a follow-up, employees fix what needs to be fixed.

Follow-up steps can assume a variety of forms. In the mid-1980s, TWA ran an ad campaign aimed at showing that it was taking major steps to improve its service. The ads featured a group of quality-control/service inspectors traveling TWA incognito on a daily basis, whose job it was to arrive unannounced and to evaluate both service and adherence to procedures.

Other service establishments use "shopper services" which essentially are professional shoppers, professional hotel guests, etc. They are hired to work as typical consumers, logging their experiences for management. Intelligent use of these findings, of course, is crucial. The results can be negative (employee dismissals), or positive (improved training programs, plans to improve performance and eliminate problem areas).

Another form of follow-up relates directly to the customer. Perhaps a better example is an airport auto repair facility (Sohio Procare). I and many other travelers have found this to be a valuable service. It permits me to leave my car for repair or maintenance as I'm leaving town. Procare provides me with a business card *and* a quarter for use in calling them when I get back. I will then be met at the terminal (usually in my own repaired car), and presented with my bill for review and payment. The car is usually cleaned, repaired, and ready to go. This is certainly a convenient service, but it continues after you pay your bill and depart from the airport. Within a few days a Procare representative telephones to inquire if all maintenance and/or repairs were handled satisfactorily. I've used this service dozens of times, and my car has been ready when promised, even when I change my arrival time. In addition, I don't have to call them. They will *follow up* and, if necessary, take care of any problems—a win-win situation.

Obviously, there are many effective follow-up techniques, and what is appropriate for your particular service offering may require special planning. But once a plan is devised, it *must* be implemented. The procedure must be clearly communicated to those who will implement it, and then you must follow up to make sure it is done. Unless all these steps are taken, all the promises of your promotional ad will only lead to creating a more cynical consumer.

You can never assume that your *point-of-encounter*

employees have received your message. If you do, you may be faced with the following scenario:

> A special presentation of the new promotion is provided to senior management.
>
> After listening to the presentation, the majority of senior management think it is just great, and pass the written (unread) information to junior management.
>
> These, in turn, "assume" that the field managers will read it, ask questions, and provide a detailed presentation to all supervisors of *point-of-encounter* employees.
>
> What actually happens is that the supervisors merely scan the information and pass it along to the *point-of-encounter* employees. Result: no implementation or, at best, poor implementation because there was no follow-up.

Of course, there is no foolproof method for follow-up, but what seems to work best is direct communication with the actual *point-of-encounter* employees. If, for some reason, this is not possible, it may pay to invest in training personnel, either face-to-face or by video and plan for review of the materials on a regular basis. Reminders can be sent, spot audits/checks performed, rewards given to those who perform well, and retraining provided to those who need it. (If your retrained employee is still not performing as required, recognize that you do not have a *point-of-encounter* employee; you have a "pig that can't learn to dance," and get one that can.

Communications and Follow-up Tips

1. Make a list of all *point-of-encounter* positions.

2. Establish a personal "communications" calendar, scheduling specific frequent dates to deliver your messages to these key people.

3. Consider delivering these messages either in person, by video tape, or in writing (in that order).

4. Make sure all of your *point-of-encounter* employees clearly understand that their personal contact with customers represents the most critical element to conveying a good service impression.

5. Listen. Listen. Listen.

6. Communicate the "right" way by *showing* the employees—not merely telling them.

7. Record and remember names, incidents, from your own employee encounters.

8. "Re-touch" those you can with a call or a note.

9. Be sincere.

10. Repeat all steps regularly. (Employee turnover is the most critical factor in diluting your message and communications in general.)

STEP X

BEGIN AGAIN

For a number of reasons, this step is perhaps the most difficult. First, to some extent, having to repeat may imply that you have not been successful with the previous nine steps. Second, you need to go back to determine if, indeed, you did not succeed with any of the actions taken. If so, you will need to fix it or replace it. Here is an example of what has to be done.

ANATOMY OF A PLAN

A number of years ago, when frequent traveler programs were sweeping the airline and hotel industries, one company decided to launch its own program. The *recognition* step took about three years to implement, as some members of senior management were reluctant to enter what was referred to as the "giveaway game." This perspective was reflected in the argument that was given: "We don't need these damn promotions. All we need to do is give travelers the service they expect." But as market share dwindled, it became increasingly evident that the company was alone in this view, and a less-than-enthusiastic decision was made to launch a program.

Next came the *identification* process, which included not only the typical awards aspect, but "service" benefits. Both were based on a thorough identification of what the consumer wanted, plus an analysis of three years of the competition's history (or rather leadership). Because of this firm's higher level of service and higher rates, it became evident that their program could offer the most service benefits and highest "payout" in the industry. They also recognized that, because of their relatively small size and location/distribution limitations, the program would have to be very good to attract and maintain new business. In addition, this initial effort would have to pass the acid test of senior management skepticism.

A comprehensive *plan of action* was developed. They had to avoid being a look-alike program by using a unique advertising and promotional plan. They began by *reallocating* both financial and personnel *resources* to make the program a success. Advertising and promotional dollars were *reallocated*, and production budgets established. Staff were reassigned not only to develop the program, but to make it the number-one *priority* for everyone in marketing.

To overcome any field resistance, a comprehensive *training* plan was set in place. This started at the top through briefings on the program for senior management. It included *recruiting* teams of trainers, made up of internal personnel. Each training team was then assigned an operating location with instructions to personally visit and conduct training sessions for all three shifts.

The *communications* step included instructional memoranda and verbal explanations for all personnel involved, preparation and distribution of a training manual, a slide presentation for the trainers and management, and even a "leave-behind" video tape for new employees who might have missed the training.

Final *follow-up* memoranda were sent out both prior to the launch date, and periodically thereafter. Follow-up phone calls were made to each unit's "program coordinator" to make sure that all training and promotional materials had arrived and to answer any questions.

The massive program launch was flagged with bells, whistles, and buttons appropriate to a new promotion, and within days, hundreds—and then thousands—of customers had taken them up on their offer and "joined the club." Naturally, all were pretty excited as enrollment continued to grow. Marketing kept the "hype" going, convinced they had a winner. And from a marketing perspective, they did!

On the down side, within six weeks, problems began to surface. First, the valued consumers who had enrolled were voicing more and more complaints about service benefits that were not being honored and about award points not being provided at check-out. Second, the cynical senior management contingent that originally had opposed the program was saying that business wasn't that much better. Third, letters were being sent to the president indicating that some units didn't seem to know much, if anything, about the program. This continued for the better part of the first year after launch.

WHAT WENT WRONG:
ANALYSIS OF THE STEPS IN RETROSPECT

What had gone wrong? Where were the trouble spots? Why were these problems recurring nine months into the program? Was there a pattern? These were the questions that consistently emerged as discussions with negative members of management grew more heated. In order to answer the questions all had to go back to the steps:

- *Recognition.* In the initial step, a major oversight was not analyzing why the firm had been three years late in launching the program. The focus had been on the consumer and the opportunity to go after market share. In essence, the recognition process had been only proactive and externally focused. It should also have addressed the internal situation, seeking to be reactive to what would be discovered.

- *Identification.* A major internal area also was missed in the identification process. Although the opportunities for providing superior service and award benefits and the need for good training had been identified, the depth of negativism by senior management had not been assessed. Analysis revealed that problems were mainly in one half of the operating units. The other half was reaping the benefits of the promotional program and, in the process, incurring far fewer complaints. At the top of the complaint list were three units that reported directly to the senior operating officer who had been most vociferously opposed to such promotional programs. The other two units reported to operating officers who worked for the same senior officer. And business was flat or down in all these units.

In summary, the problem had been identified, the source(s) located. Further investigation revealed that, in spite of the plethora of communications and what was perceived as a strong and growing program, not everyone was on board. Unit manager perspective was influenced by negative senior leadership. *Point-of-encounter* employees said, "The vice president told our manager that we didn't have time for, nor did we need to worry about this marketing program. . . ."

- *Plan of Action.* What type of action do you take to solve a problem of such magnitude? Inevitably, the wrong one—confrontation. Most organizations are open or healthy enough to withstand confrontation. Most presidents don't want it, but when it happens, they don't want to take sides. So what happens? The conflicting sides throw salvos at each other instead of at the competition. The commander in chief stands aside, temporarily paralyzed by the failure of his "generalship." The net result; internal strife, while the competitors march on.

Of course, there are other plans of action for addressing a problem of this magnitude, such as sabotage and hiring a referee. But those might not produce results, so it was decided to *begin again—*

to reallocate, prioritize, recruit, retrain, and communicate.

- *Reallocation.* The first step was to reallocate additional funds to relaunch the program *internally.* It was decided to develop a new communications and training program for all *point-of-encounter* employees.

- *Prioritization.* A task force was assembled to address the retraining of those who needed it, as well as to communicate the importance of personal involvement by *point-of-encounter* personnel. All had to be made to understand that the program was part of the job on which they would be evaluated. This had to be done in a way that would overcome the prior negativism that had been conveyed by senior management. Not only was retraining focused on procedures (critical for the consumer), but, more importantly, on a positive attitude toward involvement.

- *Training.* There was no feasible way to achieve this retraining through writing or in person. Strong negative perceptions cannot be eliminated with memos or pep talks, especially if this involves criticism. You have to recruit strong players and wage psychological warfare. This means you must risk breaking the state of paralysis of your leader to see which way he will go.

- *Recruiting.* When you want to win, you recruit the best. "Who" and, more importantly, "how" you recruit under such circumstances is vital.

Start by thoroughly reviewing the job that needs to be done in order to ascertain the type of person who will be best suited. Review your problems by reading complaint letters and talking directly to those who have complained. Armed with this knowledge, go out and recruit the very best people with the skills, personality, and experience to solve the problems.

Communications. It may come as no surprise that problems identified in complaint letters can be the result of apathy by front line employees and/or poor internal communications. The following complaint letter illustrates the problem:

Dear Mr. President:

As a loyal customer and frequent user of your units, I was most pleased to join your new club for loyal customers. I was particularly pleased to learn that I could receive the outstanding service benefits of your program. You can imagine my disappointment when your employees said, "We don't honor that program," and yet at another unit, I was told, "We don't know anything about that program." Needless to say, I will no longer use your services nor will my thousands of employees.

Sincerely yours,
____ , President

P.S. Your program is great. It's too bad your units are so poorly trained-operated.

It doesn't take the intelligence of a rocket scientist to recognize that receipt of a half-dozen such letters might unparalyze your president.

So the fuse is lit! Now comes *your point of encounter*. It entails a different form of confrontation—"conflict solution." It is your own memo to your own president.

> Mr. President, as you may be aware, we have a communications problem with our *point-of-encounter* employees. We know the problem is more severe in selected units and can certainly understand why this program may be causing problems. However, our valued and loyal customers are responding to the program and we are also getting new customers. We need to fix this problem by recognizing that we have fallen short in our communications, and should now begin again. We believe a presidential video message to *point-of-encounter* employees is the best way to get all those involved on the same track. It will reduce complaints and help us keep our valued customers. We would also like you, as president, to communicate with other top executives through advertising in the major media, including T.V.
>
> We have checked your schedule and can shoot the video tapes this Friday at 10:00 A.M. We'll need to do that to make the media deadlines.

From the president's perspective, he can now blame some*thing* rather than some*one* for the problem;

i.e., poor communications. Further, it gives him an opportunity to break out of his "paralysis" and move into action. He will be viewed as leading his troops into the fray.

The video directed at the employees urges them to carry out "his" program. It goes on to what is and is not to be done, and closes with, "I look forward to personally experiencing this program when I see you at your unit."

- *Follow-up.* There is still more to be done. Occasional letters from consumers are shared with the employees—both positive and negative. Additional video tapes of presidential messages are shown. More "thank you" notes are sent to *point-of-encounter* employees and even to the negative staff members! All of this is done so there is no need to begin again until it is *recognized* that the program had died a natural death. When that happens, of course, you *are* ready to "begin again" with the Ten Steps to Service Success!

Recap of the Ten Steps to Service Success

  I. *Recognition*—Knowing that there is a service opportunity and/or problem as the *points of encounter.*
 II. *Identification*—Determining what they are.
III. *Plan of Action*—Developing the plan required to capitalize on an opportunity or deal with a problem.

IV. *Reallocation*—Finding the financial and/or human resources to execute the plan.

V. *Prioritization*—Placing execution of the plan *at the top of the list.*

VI. *Training*—Ensuring thorough preparation of those who are charged with taking action at *points of encounter.*

VII. *Recruiting*—Finding the very best persons for execution of the plan as well as for *point-of-encounter* positions.

VIII. *Communications*—Conveying every aspect of your plan(s) accurately, thoroughly, and convincingly to *all* employees, with special focus on front-line personnel.

IX. *Follow-up*—Monitoring of new recruits, training (and retraining), effectiveness of communications and again, most importantly, *point-of-encounter* employees.

X. *Begin Again*—Periodically review all the processes—beginning with the steps of recognition and identification.

III

Encounters of a Service Kind

Donald Trump tells the story of how his firm completed the skating rink in Central Park in three months, after the New York City government had been at it for years. When asked how he did it, he responded, "There wasn't one day I didn't check on the progress we were making." And Trump didn't just telephone to check; he was there—on the job. The point is simply this: You have to demonstrate leadership by *doing*. You must be capable of directing everyone involved to be successful at the *point of encounter*:

THE KEYS TO
ENCOUNTER SUCCESS
FOR MANAGEMENT
IN THE SERVICES
INDUSTRY

*E*nvision The Opportunity

*N*otice All The Areas

*C*onsider Your Own Checklist

*O*rganize Your Resources

*U*se Your Authority

*N*ow Is The Time To Train All

*T*arget Your Hiring

*E*mployees At The Front Line

*R*eview The Key Result Areas

*S*tart Over Again!

FOR MANAGEMENT IN THE SERVICE INDUSTRY

There are generic keys that are applicable to virtually every service industry manager/management.

1. Envision the opportunity at your disposal to improve profits. You know why your service organization stays in business. Regardless of all the flashy theories that say to turn the pyramid upside down, concentrate more on the customer and less on the plan. As a manager, you cannot afford to lose sight of the reason you're employed—*profits!* As a renowned consultant friend of mine so bluntly states: "Profits are like breathing; if we don't breathe, we are dead."

2. Notice all the areas within your service offering where you can increase "oxygen intake." Review every component of your service offering and ask the right questions: Are we pricing correctly for the quality/value perception of our service? Can we raise the perception by improving the quality, and consequently getting higher, better prices and/or market share? What can we do to better control inventories and cash flow? Many examples demonstrate this concept of increasing profit by upgrading services, raising prices, and getting a greater market share. The key factor is that you, as a manager, must "notice" the specific step(s) at your disposal.

3. Consider developing your own checklist of inspection items, but do it from the customer's

perspective. Sure, audit forms, checklists, reports, and so on, exist within your service organization, but is consideration given to the customer's reactions?

Take the example of the company that hires shoppers to evaluate how well the company is doing meeting customers' needs.* You can do the same kind of inspection either yourself or by hiring others to experience your service firsthand. You can start with telephone inquiries to see how your toll-free number is operating, then follow through to the actual purchase of goods or services. From this research, you can develop your own relevant consumers' perspective checklist for your managers to apply in the same way.

Make sure the checklist is as detailed as possible. For example, let's assume the service offering is a business with parking lots, elevators, and physical grounds, such as a hospital or hotel. The "auditor" type checklist perspective might read as follows:

- Is the parking lot laid out to provide for the maximum number of vehicles?

- Is energy being conserved by shutting down excess elevator cars during off-peak hours?

- Are the exterior grounds designed for minimum maintenance and upkeep?

* One major word of caution: You must also analyze findings and take action to improve your service offerings. *Telling* your customers through advertising that you're checking on your employees is one thing (and not very much), but actually *doing* this and taking action is what matters.

Conversely, the consumers' perspective would ask about those same three areas as follows:

- Is the parking lot cleaned before and after peak usage, and are all lights inspected regularly to ensure that the customer feels safe?

- Are the elevators regulated to provide maximum service at all hours, and are they clean and odor-free?

- Are the exterior grounds clean and the shrubbery and lawns well maintained?

4. Organize the resources of your personnel daily to address the jobs that are most important to your customers. You must be sure not to allow anything to interfere with the "set" procedures. It is your *point of encounter* with employees that will convey the urgency of providing ongoing excellent service to your customers.

5. Use your authority to direct the focus of your entire team on the items that are critical to service success *and* profit. Dr. Peter Drucker coined the term "KRA," or *Key Result Areas.* Make sure that everyone on your management team *and* each of your front-line employees knows and understands your firm's KRAs. Do not hesitate to inform everyone that these are key items and, therefore, are the major reasons for successful service. Let your employees know that providing correct service and having a correct attitude are *why* they are being paid. Even if employees are

performing keypunch or data entry functions when they accept reservations, selling insurance over the telephone, admit someone into a hospital, or accept an application for a new bank account, they must understand that they are being paid to "service" the customer, *not* to punch keys or enter data.

6. Now is the time to be sure that every one of your employees knows exactly what to do. If they do not know, you must provide the resources to correct the situation.

There are two options at your disposal. You can pull the employees from customer contact and send them through a formal training program. Or, you can provide on-the-job training by "pairing" the untrained with the trained employees. But when doing this, take into consideration that, if the point of encounter is a busy one, whether there is enough time for training. Think about the consumer at the Newark Airport counter watching those employees stare at computer terminal screens. With the time-lag created by on-the-job training does the traveler really expect his or her name to pop up quickly? Will the agent ever look up and make *eye contact*?

7. Target your hiring and review your *point-of-encounter* employees as carefully as possible. These employees are more important than anyone else in your company. They are the people who either satisfy or lose customers, make or lost money. Actually, they are much more important than you are! If you don't believe it, take a day off, or even a week. Does your firm lose money or go out of

business? But what happens when your only ser-vice/*point-of-encounter* employee is out sick for a week and there is no backup?

8. Employees at the front line can either sink your ship or help you sail to success. It is essential that you listen to these employees and ask them the right questions. Be sure they understand the KRAs and why they are entrusted to execute these steps. Doing so on a regular basis is one of the few ways to quickly assess your front line's depth of understanding of the critical issues.

9. Review the KRAs with managers and front-line employees daily. By doing so, you reaffirm to them the importance of focusing on these critical items and make certain that they are following through. There is no better example than that set by management itself. Of course, if management is indifferent about these key areas, there is no worse example.

10. Start over again at Key One. Remember it is al-ways possible to identify additional opportunities or refine an approach for solving a problem.

These ten keys require either the individual man-ager or the management team to go beyond the *point of encounter* with employees in reinforcing the process until it becomes second nature to everyone in the service business. The only way to overcome the consumer's cynicism, and the only way to achieve a front line that is capable of executing and going beyond the *point of encounter* is to recognize the com-mon denominator—leadership.

Just as there are steps your company (and management) must take, there are steps your employees must take to ensure customer satisfaction. No matter what type of service you provide, there are several keys to the effective execution that will create recognition among consumers that your firm goes beyond the *point-of-encounter*.

1. *Expectations.* Recognize that you must never deliver a service that falls short of what the customer or potential customer expects for the price they're paying. Meeting or exceeding customer expectations is what ultimately determines the level of customer satisfaction. Expectation levels in the *mind* of the consumer are influenced by: the price you charge; their prior experience with your service offering; their prior experience with your competition; and what you promise in your advertising or sales message. Meeting *customer expectations* is absolutely critical to repeat business.

2. *Never blame the customer.* While some may argue with this categorical statement, you cannot lose by practicing it. The customer *is* always right, even if he or she is not! Simply stated: Let the customer win! That doesn't mean you should allow the customer to take advantage of you. This means that your employees must understand that they have the flexibility and authority to bend policy when needed to satisfy a customer.

Most surveys show that less than 5% of customers will actually take the time to complain about the service received. However, these same surveys also show that almost 25% are less than satisfied with that service. And this percentage grows dramatically when customers become increasingly cynical as a result of poor experiences with other companies offering the same type of service. When this occurs, two things can happen. (1) If you insist that your employees adhere so strictly to policy that customers are not allowed to "feel" they have won, you will lose 100% of those cynical consumers. (2) If you have instilled in your employees the "let the customers *feel* they have won" philosophy, you will retain (and actually *build*) the loyalty of these customers.

GOING BEYOND EXPECTATIONS

Stouffer Hotels ran a frequent traveler/guest promotion that involved awarding loyal customers with U.S. Savings Bonds. The value of the bonds was based on the number of nights the customer was lodged in its hotels. Since even the upscale frequent traveler may not fully grasp an offering at times, they did have some complaints, usually from those who did not understand that they had to send in their bond redemption certificates, which had been presented to them at checkout. Stouffer had to make choices of how to handle the matter when someone sent in a redemption form for bonds that either did not include bond certificates or did not include the correct number of certificates for the bond value being requested.

One way would have been to follow the controller's policy and send a form letter which, in essence would have said, "Dear Valued Customer: Thanks for playing our game. Unfortunately, you're too stupid to follow the rules. Try again!" Instead when such "mistakes" were discovered by the accounting department, the redemption form was sent to the marketing department. The procedure then was to try to trace the guest's history of stays at the hotels. If the appropriate number of stays was confirmed, the bonds were issued. (Obviously it checked any future requests to avoid duplicate issuance.) If it could not confirm that the guest had stayed the required number of nights, one of two things was done. If the deficiency in redemption certificates was minor, Stouffer simply issued the bond with a note saying, "Here is your bond, dear valued customer. Enclosed is another copy of the rules. Thank you for staying with Stouffer Hotels and please stay with us again." If the deficiency was substantial or if no certificates had been provided with the redemption form, Stouffer would telephone its valued customer and indicate that it was anxious to expedite the award, explaining the problem and asking if redemption certificates had been received. If the response was that they had been lost or misplaced, the customer was then asked for specific information regarding their stays.

Stouffer *never* made customers feel as if they were being "blamed." The end result was extraordinary—letters to the president, repeat business, and thank you calls from the customer. In essence, Stouffer was telling its valued customers (who happen to be senior business leaders), that "we value you" and "we want to keep you happy." Even more gratifying were the phone calls, that were received regularly from many of these same customers telling of their good and/or bad experiences. They weren't requesting refunds or asking that specific actions be taken; they were sharing their experiences with someone they felt would take care of their "problems." A few CEOs even called after each stay and said, in effect: "Just wanted to let you know how your hotel or resort was doing . . . will keep you posted after my next stay."

3. Clear communication with customers is essential to problem resolution at the *point of encounter* or purchase. Your employees must be able to tell customers precisely what they need and want to know or do. This is especially critical when you're involved in a promotional offer. After all, that is *why* the new customer has come to you in the first place. Make sure that everyone who has customer-contact responsibility *and* supervisors are thoroughly knowledgeable about all aspects of the promotion. If necessary, provide written communiqués and training videos. Augment these with in-person training sessions, and do so in a timely manner. *Never* start a promotion before all employees have received complete information and thorough instructions. And always provide a central resource for clarification should questions arise.

4. Organize your procedures to reduce the *time* it takes to purchase your service offering. The number-one peeve of today's consumer of services is "standing in line." You must review and then revise your procedures to eliminate or at least shorten the time spent waiting in line. If the nature of your service precludes total elimination

of waiting time, develop alternative plans to "fill the time." This can be in the form of a customer service representative who pre-processes the customers or socializes with them. A video entertainment or informational display will attract the customer and fill the waiting time.

One national department store came up with an innovative plan to keep the waiting customers occupied: at check-in for the service, they are provided with a "beeper" to carry while browsing through the store. The customer is cautioned not to leave the premises (because the range of the "beeper" is limited) and told to return to the service area when the beeper sounds. Not only did this minimum-cost procedure eliminate long lines, the need for nonproductive square footage, and tedious waiting for unhappy customers, it *in*creased the potential for in-house sales.

If you're cynical about such "fillers," mount a fixed-base exercise bike and do nothing but pedal for five minutes—no reading, no radio, no TV. Then repeat the process reading a book, listening to the radio, or watching TV. Those five minutes will seem a lot shorter.

5. *Undo* what the customer has done to himself. When customers discover that they are in the wrong, always avoid embarrassing them. The employee must be polite, empathetic, and tactful so that your customers "save face."

6. *Never* use business jargon that is unfamiliar to your customer. You cannot assume that even those who are in the other businesses use the same terminology as you.

7. Trade-off time management is essential in personal-contact situations. Each *point of encounter* must be analyzed and a determination made as to whether the strategy should be to go for "optimum speed" or special "personal attention." For example, when there is no line, and "Friendly Henry" decides to mosey up to your employee with a "Hi! How are you'all on this beautiful day?" your employee should take the circumstances into account. He or she should not be "overtrained" to process Henry impersonally with nary a glance, eyes glued to the CRT terminal, and so rapidly as to be perceived cold or rude. On the other hand, when "Harried Harriet" steps up to the counter with credit card and pen in hand, the employee should realize that Harriet is trying for an Olympic record in moving through that *point-of-encounter*.

8. Employee job performance criteria for all those in *point-of-encounter* positions, be they face to face, or over the phone, should clearly focus on execution of service with efficiency *and* politeness. This is what it's all about, and *point-of-encounter* employees must *know* that performing their job properly is what they are being paid for!

9. Reduce time where service is *expected* to be fast. Fast and efficient service leads to satisfaction, especially today. In essence, cynical consumers' negative conditioning has led them to expect long lines and/or slow, inefficient service. Beat that expectation! Provide faster service and you will convert the cynical consumer into one who is more than satisfied.

10. Sincere appreciation should be expressed at virtually all *points of encounter*—not just at the time of purchase. This must be instilled in every contact-point employee. This will ensure reinforcement of the perception that the customer is truly valued.

Recap of the Keys to Encounter Service Success with Today's Cynical Consumer

---

*E*xpectations Must Be Met
*N*ever Blame The Customer
*C*lear Communications
*O*rganize To Reduce Time
*U*ndo What The Customer Has Done To Himself/Herself
*N*ever Embarrass The Customer
*T*rade-Off Time Management Is Essential
*E*mployee Job Performance Criteria
*R*educe Service Time
*S*incere Appreciation Expressed

IV

Beyond the *Points of Encounter*

In the marketplace rampant with cynicism, it is often necessary for even superior companies to reach beyond the excellence achieved by their *point-of-encounter* employees. No matter how perfect the execution, there are other factors which require a broader perspective. This must include: (1) an ongoing assessment of the needs and expectations of the consumer; (2) packaging of your service offering and your promises to meet the identified needs and expectations of the marketplace; (3) maintaining a "success" perception through examples of performance while conducting a realistic competitive and self-positioning analysis; and (4) defining and designing valid and productive networking versus the nonsensical association games.

In today's marketplace, there is a "blurring" of choices for the consumer. The cause may be the sheer amount of competition, or the consumer's conditioned cynicism and indifference. Even if your service is excellent, other competitors are probably offering a similar level of service. This means that to be "the" successful entity, you must go beyond the *points of encounter* experienced at all other like businesses (either in actual performance or in your packaging) to the creation of the perception that declares, "Mr. and Ms. Consumer, in spite of the apparent equity in competition, this is why you should purchase and/or use *my* service offering." You must distinguish your *message and your service* from that of your competitors.

This means fine-tuning the ten steps to service success so that your service *is* superior to all the rest.

To achieve this fine-tuning and to establish a basis for creation of a distinctive perception, you must start by focusing on the aspects of that consumer's "needs" and "expectations" as they relate to your particular service offering.

NEEDS AND EXPECTATIONS

After over 20 years in the service industry, I am still amazed when, in discussions with other firms, I learn how little their management knows about the service needs of their consumers. Understanding the needs of your customers should be job number one, yet I believe that the project vs. people mentality has many counterparts in other sectors of the service industry. One is the "bytes, mainframe, and capacity" mentality, which pays attention to needs, but mainly those of management information system (MIS) personnel. This is the group that is funded from the fastest-growing line in your expense budget—those who produce reams of reports and very neat computer displays telling you how bad things are as a result of spending so much on the needs.

Another type lives and thrives on the introspective "blame and change" mentality. Here, the focus is on the needs of the biggest or newest ego to arrive on the scene. This type is equally effective at spending on the wrong, nonconsumer-oriented items. They can be even more dangerous because they "blame" the previous person for lack of success while expediting "change" that reflects their own perspectives rather than the customer's.

I'll skip the multitude of computer-related examples that illustrate how not knowing the needs of your customers often results in not having any, and just mention the story of one restaurateur who blindly invested over $500,000 to establish the finest French restaurant in the heart of an eastern city. And I mean blindly! A simple analysis of the market would have revealed that he had chosen a commuter city—one that turned into a ghost town after 6:00 P.M. Second, consumers in that area were not accustomed to high prices. Third, the main market was business lunches that took an hour or less. This fancy French restaurant needed a couple of hours to serve a complete lunch. And, fourth, the menu failed to include beef! (The chef specialized in fish and veal.) Needless to say, the investment went down the kitchen drain.

Identification of the needs of your potential market is essential. How can the promises made in your promotion be accurate (other than by luck) if you don't know those needs? What has this to do with the *points of encounter*? Because the very first exposure to your service offering is extraordinarily important for a number of reasons. The first impression will be a lasting one and extremely difficult to change, because it establishes your customers' expectations.

Take the famous Federal Express commercial featuring the fast-talking character. That made a very strong statement: "It absolutely positively will get there overnight." The promise of prompt delivery catered to consumers' needs and expectations. Federal Express clearly and dramatically distinguished its service offering from the rest, and at the same time was able to justify the higher cost as compared to slower delivery services. From day one they focused on the *point of encounter*. They pick up from the consumer (unlike the Postal Service) and deliver to the recipient the very next day. This is what they claimed to do and it is exactly what they *have* done—something almost beyond cynical consumers' expectations.

Think about some of these examples of needs, responses, and meeting of consumer expectations: Consider the traveler calling for reservations to a hotel that allows the telephone to ring 16 times. What will be the expectation of that hotel's service at the *points of encounter*? Will the traveler even want to experience the service? When United Airlines' service level declined in the mid-'80s, consumers reacted. They did not care about UAL's problems with its employees. They did care that those employees, enraged at management, provided a reduced service. They cared and reacted because their cynicism had been reinforced with the slogan, "Fly the Friendly Skies."

Ironically, United had spent millions promoting that catchy phrase, only to have it backfire. While *advertising* had stressed the needs of the consumer, management's perspective focused on its own needs and on its employees. Friendly indeed, was the cynical reaction. The result: lost market share.

How does the consumer feel about Allstate Insurance's slogan, "You're in Good Hands"? Probably good when the proper amount is paid promptly; surely bad when the settlement is late and deemed inadequate. Allstate's extensive promotion of their slogan and symbol caters to the need of the consumer for prompt help when an accident occurs.

American Express offers another example of building a service expectation based on the promise to meet needs with its variety of lost-traveler's-check commercials. Here the need for security when traveling is certainly identified. The dangers are explicitly spelled out and the assurance that American Express will be there when needed is powerfully dramatized.

Does it work? Obviously yes, since American Express is huge and successful. But why does it work so well? Because the company has identified a need, promised to meet the expectations of its customers, and through intensive training of its *point-of-encounter* personnel, lives up to its promises.

Researchers are busy surveying consumers to determine what they want and need in terms of service offerings. They also try to find out what consumers do *not* want. The following are some of their "profound" findings: prompt service, no hassles with returns or exchanges, competent help, convenience, good value (quality at a fair price), friendly personnel, and no lines.

The following chart illustrates some consumer expectations and the outcomes when they are met—and when they are not.

Armed with such findings, service firms can begin to formulate plans to eliminate "cynical consumer expectations" at *points of encounter*. If a firm has the desire and confidence in its ability to fulfill promises, it should adopt the approach of Federal Express—tell prospective customers that you know they are cynical, but you promise to meet their expectations. By making the promise you go out on a limb. You are even more motivated to live up to the promise because when you do, you have gained satisfied customers, and if you don't, you have lost them—forever.

Packaging the Promises

Both Federal Express and American Express succeeded in packaging their promises dramatically and fulfilling them at the *points of encounter*. As a result, their consumers have been converted from cynics to loyalists.

What promises should you make? How should they be packaged? In the service industry you're mostly dealing with intangibles. There is no "product" to display in an eye-catching package. The service industry has made considerable strides in the presentation of its offerings, as noted, but attracting customers is just the beginning; you must be sure to execute well at the *points of encounter*. The competitor is out there using the same or perhaps better packaging, and trying to meet customers' needs. What, then, can make the difference? Attracting consumers to your service is basic, then keeping them by offering enhancements to your service.

You can never assume you're so good at what you do that no one can take your customers from you. Some consider lost market share to competitors resulting from packaging (as compared to actual service differences at the *points of encounter*), a "cheap" or unfair victory. The truth is often that the competitor found a new point of encounter with the consumer to exploit and won fair and square.

In the mid-1980s Embassy Suites was conceived

NEEDS, CYNICISM, AND SATISFACTION CHART

Expressed Need (Research Finding)	Cynical Consumer Expectation	Satisfaction Level (Needs met beyond expectation)	Dissatisfaction Level (Needs met below expectation)
1. Prompt service	Second or third in line	No line (Immediate service)	Sixth on line (long wait) or required to change lines after wait
2. No hassles with returns or exchanges	Argument, review, or inspection	Full refund or replacement (no hassles)	Loss of argument, partial refund or lengthy referral for resolution (even if favorable)
3. Competent help	Average to incompetent (will have to go to Supv. or other)	Gets all answers and help by one person (the first one)	Surly, rude, or very poorly trained help (no back-up)
4. Convenient	Some but limited inconvenience	Right there, no walk, by phone, no forms; signature only	Major inconveniences: Only at downtown store Only thru the catalog Must complete the forms
5. Value	Cheap price/ limited services ── or ── Expensive/ some services	Good level of services — Full services/extras	Cheap price/no service — Very limited services

and launched by the Holiday Corporation (later renamed Promus Corporation). In the lodging industry this company had been offering middle-of-the-market product and low-service levels with its other brands. The upscale, high-service level lodging chains initially viewed Embassy Suites' offering with the typical snobbery of the project vs. people mentality. Some proclaimed it would be an economic disaster. "You can't provide a suite for the price of one room." Others said, "So, they offer a suite. We offer more services." And, "Can you imagine using 'Garfield the Cat' to launch your entry into the upscale lodging market?" What happened? Embassy Suites beat the competition by offering a new product/service that met the needs (in fact, newly important needs due to changing pyschographic trends) of the consumer. Embassy Suites worked from the market and economic perspective, gaining instant brand-recognition by breaking the mold and using Garfield. While many within the industry scoffed at Garfield, the mass of consumers who wanted to be treated like "fat cats" had a suite, did not pay a fortune, and avoided all the snobbish chains. They've switched to and stay with Embassy Suites.

In air transportation, Peoples Express found a need in the opposite direction—providing "pure value" in the form of inexpensive air fare with minimal services. "You pay for your meals, drinks, etc. and get a seat for a low price." But the plan went out of control. Sometimes the attraction of cheap seats resulted in chaos at terminals and departure gates when flights were oversold. Sometimes became frequently; canceled flights, equipment problems, and air traffic delays drained the value and left passengers in seats that gave them a "pain in the butt." Peoples Express fell apart at all the major *points of encounter*: at the reservation desk, at the terminal, at check-in, at the gate, at boarding, on board, and at the baggage claim. Even to those whose needs were minimal with expectations limited to a seat on a plane, Peoples Express failed to fulfill its promises.

We all receive many service solicitations by mail, especially from insurance companies, brokerage firms, banks, and credit card companies. Why do we open some and discard others? Why do we respond to some and not to others? The answer usually lies in the packaging and promises. Consider how many ways 10% interest can be offered, how many types of life insurance policies can be sold, and why you do or do not respond. If the offer is timely; i.e., you're in the market for it, naturally you'll respond, but to which offer— and why? For some people, it's the packaging. You know—that embossed and gold-stamped membership card complete with your name and number. For others, it's pure price. For still others, it may be fear: "How will I pay those hospital bills?" Some people are swayed by the endorsement of trusted celebrities. What was your reason for responding to a solicitation? In all likelihood, the packaging and *point of encounter* sales pitch met your need at the time and, most importantly, succeeded in overcoming your conditioned cynicism about all that junk mail or phone calls you receive.

Recently I responded to a direct-mail solicitation from the American Automobile Association to join the AAA Plus Program. At the time I had a company car with a full expense account and all the numbers to call for help and service. So, why AAA Plus for me? A few lines of copy and some photographs caught my "needs" eye. I also had cars for my son and my wife. I lived in a northern state that is very cold in the winter, and required annual driver's license plate renewal in person—the old-time patronage game. AAA Plus perceived a need and advertised a way to meet that need, saying, in essence, "Don't worry about dead batteries or your family getting stuck in the snow. And why stand in line to pay off a politician just to get your license plate?" Well, AAA Plus got me to sign up quickly because they addressed directly my needs and overcame my ingrained cynicism. Why hadn't I responded to all the other automobile clubs' direct mail solicitations? Because AAA Plus met more of my needs, especially not having to stand in the "idiot" lines at the Motor Vehicles Bureau.

This is another example of the application of the steps to service success: meet the needs; execute at the *points of encounter*; package your service, and ensure that promises are kept as expected. I might also mention that after I mailed my check, I received a follow-up call from a AAA representative asking if I had any questions and thanking me for joining the club. *Perception and performance.*

The perception of your service offering is, to a very great extent, reflected in the packaging and promises. Now this should ring in a bell of caution, especially in the age of the cynical consumer. But if you play the perception and performance game correctly, you will overcome cynicism and win. If you don't play it right you will have a dissatisfied customer and a loss. So, what is the right way?

If your service offering is so fine-tuned that you believe you can promise a great deal and deliver 100% on your promises, you can take the risk of going all the way—and you may win. On the other hand, if you promise a little less, and deliver a little more, you are practically assured of winning. You will have created the perception of meeting the consumers' needs and then delivered that "unexpected extra."

Here is a simple illustration of "how to lose." Your advertised promises to the cynical consumer might go something like this:

> The Superior Service Company will maintain your business premises by cleaning carpets and washing all windows weekly, picking up all visible trash daily, waxing all floors nightly, polishing all metal surfaces twice a week; replacing all defective lighting nightly, and since you are our valued customer, will replace any flowers or shrubs that are not 100% healthy—free of charge. In addition, the Superior Service Company agrees to mow all lawns and weed the flower beds twice weekly.

For the management of a supermarket or an office complex, or a restaurant owner, this offer appears to be exactly what is needed to maintain the desired first-class image. The impression is that the service company really knows its business down to the smallest detail.

But how fast will Superior Service Company lose the account(s) if it doesn't deliver on even one of its promises? Mighty fast! You just can't make promises that you don't keep and expect to keep customers. Yet, we see it every day in the service industry—offers such as "no lines," "no waiting," "the lowest price," "fastest service." But don't forget those asterisks: "fly to Denver for only $69*," "deluxe weekend suites only $49*," "$100,000 coverage* only $19.95**." The small print noted by the asterisk on the $69 offer says: "Tuesday after 9 pm; one way; 27-day advance reservation required; penalty for cancellation." The asterisk on the $49 offer says: "Saturday night during December only (excludes the 29th, 30th, and 31st); per person double occupancy required; 30-day advance reservation; no children or pets." The asterisk in the insurance offer says: "Accidental death caused by being hit or struck by a moving aircraft while walking on the beach (Pacific Ocean only)." And the double asterisk on the $19.95 offer means: "Down payment!" Obviously, once you're into the asterisk syndrome, you're on your way to the consumer disappointment scenario.

Now for an example of how to win by promising to meet a need that is followed by delivery beyond expectations. The advertisement: "Enjoy a luxury weekend: fine accommodations for two; airport pickup and complimentary continental breakfast for two; $99 per night." Visualize the consumers' reactions when they (1) are picked up at the airport by a chauffeured limousine (versus the hotel van); (2) are provided a suite (versus a standard room); (3) discover a welcome note along with a chilled bottle of good champagne in the room (not promised); (4) find that they can have a full breakfast served in bed at no extra cost; and (5) receive a departing gift before the limousine ride back to the airport. Satisfied customers and repeat business? You bet!

No, this is not an extreme example of how to win. Such service is not out of the ordinary for most hotels.

Their limousines are usually just waiting around anyway, and the cost of champagne is minimal. The suites would probably be empty, and the cost of breakfast is also negligible. Let's graphically recap the perceptions and performance formulas for winning and losing.

Perception and Performance Principle

Promise to meet needs → Exceed Promise → Win.
Promise to meet/exceed expectations → Deliver 99% or Less → Lose

or

Promise 85-95% → Deliver 100%+ → Win
Promise 100% → Deliver 85-95% → Lose

Obviously you can stack the deck in your favor by using the "surprise" technique. Consumers come to believe that they will be getting something for nothing when they use your service. The trick is not to advertise the "extras"—let them be a surprise. The surprise you offer can be determined easily from an evaluation of all your service offerings.

While on the subject of "winning" I offer a guideline for everyone in the service business. But before I do so, I want to point out that I have not focused very much on such attitudes as "killing the competitor," "annihilating the enemy," or other analogies to marketing warfare. The reason is simple: If you're

Proctor & Gamble and your enemy is Colgate Palmolive or some other large company, your size will enable you to engage in warfare. You also know that although you won't win every time, you have staying power, and you can afford to try to "shoot down" the enemy. However, based on what I've witnessed in the service business, most companies would be far more successful if they concentrated on their own business and avoided the debilitating effects of warfare with others. The reason is obvious, and I've seen it happen time and again. Many service businesses that lack needed savvy for competitive warfare tend to "shoot themselves in the foot" every time they "open fire."

This can be either devastating to the business or it may result in a great opportunity. Having seen the results of the self-inflicted wound, the business can turn its efforts toward making each "potential-customer interest" situation into a firm sale, and/or generating repeat business and customer loyalty. In this way they would be far ahead of the game—and their competitors. Such "victories" would outweigh any possible advantage achieved through "warfare."

Yet, very little energy is spent in this area of training, which involves communicating a very basic principle—the one every service business should remember—let the customer win! I know this sounds simplistic, but I assure you it is not. For the customer to win, this principle must be engraved in the minds of every *point-of-encounter* employee. It doesn't mean giving away the shop; it means imparting to the customer the perception that he or she is winning.

The following suggestions may help you do this. Bear in mind that when your customer wins, you win!

Recap of Tips to let the Customer Win

- Honor expired offers/coupons presented for redemption by the customer.

- Honor promotional prices/rates even when the dates have expired.

- Upgrade your service in any way possible while retaining the original price. For example, provide a first-class seat on a short flight if the section is empty, a better room, or a better car if available.

- Provide rain checks.

- If your offer is on a first-come, first-served basis, and you are not able to honor it, provide an alternate upgrade; for example, a complimentary drink.

- Fire employees who consistently argue with consumers (even if they *are* right).

- Hire employees who smile and display empathy for your customers.

- Develop internal "Let The Customer Win" incentive awards.

- Instruct your managers to interface directly with the customer at least one shift a month.

- Provide a little "extra" surprise by empowering your *point-of-encounter* employees with the authority to act or even provide a discount.

In order to ensure the success of these winning

techniques, you may have to adjust the authority hierarchy. In general, the more authority your *point-of-encounter* employees have to let the customer win, the better. To achieve this, resources may have to be real-located. You can try incentives for the hourly em-ployee—which are the same as a bonus to the boss. If you want to be very pragmatic, the incentive can be a percentage of increased revenue. You can't lose.

Remember, "perception" is that all-important image created in the consumer's mind by your "promises" and "packaging." Execution even slightly beyond the promises made results in customer satis-faction and loyalty. And, most of all, every *point-of-encounter* employee must be instilled with the philosophy and (where possible) the authority to "Let The Customer Win." In so doing, you and your service offering become the real winners.

Networking or Nonsense

In present-day service offerings, the concept of "networking" has emerged and flourishes. In the pres-ent context, networking involves two or more busi-nesses linking their offerings, services, and/or benefits. One example is the airline, hotel, and rent-a-car network for marketing and promotion, while others are found in the banking industry through the offering of credit cards and ATM (automatic teller ma-chine) access/network agreements.

Providing wider service to the customer can be either effective and beneficial or just window dressing. For networking to be effective, the added service must enhance the attractiveness of the original offering by providing such benefits as convenience, accessibility, and monetary value. The mere meshing of company names without such concrete benefits becomes grist for the mill of the cynical consumer.

In the service business there are many examples of networking that exemplify both extremes of the spectrum. The consumer's perspective of the networking may be entirely different from that of the companies involved. For example, banks discovered that ATM networking, while a very positive convenience for the consumer, proved to be expensive and nuisance-loaded for the banks. Some banks did it to protect market share, others to survive. Very few banks were motivated to provide the service purely as a benefit to their customer.

A headline-grabbing example of the 1980s was provided by the announcement of the formation of Allegis. This networking concept was conceived as a way of incorporating United Airlines, Westin Hotels, and Hertz Rent-A-Car Company into a travel services company. While Allegis was starting up this strategic thrust, there were many on Wall Street, several members of the Board of Directors, many shareholders, and many employees who did not agree with Mr. Ferris (then-Chairman of Allegis). This combined negative force eventually disassembled the network and, in the process, Mr. Ferris left the company.

But there was much more to this network failure. From the consumer's perspective, the negatives were simple. In spite of Allegis's size, it still did not represent a large enough offering. Consumers had been turning to travel professionals for help in finding their way through the maze of changes that resulted from deregulation, Allegis felt it could meet the new needs. Unfortunately, it did not have a lot to offer when you consider the six or seven other major air carriers, hundreds of hotel chains, and several dozen rent-a-car firms in the marketplace. But Allegis believed it could affect consumer behavior to the degree required for a successful venture (brand-switching and total consumer commitment) by offering one-stop shopping and incentive awards. What they didn't recognize was that one-stop shopping hasn't as yet become the modus operandi of the majority of business travelers, except where a company uses an in-house travel planner or travel agent. Allegis defined one-stop shopping as the use of only the companies under their banner, while the consumer thought of it as having access to the services of *all* airlines, hotels, rent-a-car companies.

In spite of this particular failure, many will eventually succeed in networking the travel services business. The key will be to provide an all-encompassing service that allows the consumer the freedom to make choices in an open marketplace.

Convenience is the key. In fairness to Allegis, however, it must be stated that those who too quickly wrote off the idea never really gave the plan enough time to develop. The strategy failed not so much as a result of customer-related problems, but because there were too many enemies and too little time.

Successful networking provides *more for consumers and meets their needs.* Unsuccessful networking provides *little or no benefit to the consumer.* More importantly, the perception of the service offering must not be negative and thus increase consumer cynicism.

Will my customer benefit? Will there be a perceived enhancement of my service offering? Will it help me let the customer win? If your answer to these questions is "yes," then the network deal should be a "go." If the answer is "no" or even "maybe," in all likelihood you should discard the idea.

Ways and Means to Momentum

Desire to achieve momentum is usually the primary motivation for networking and joining co-ops. Often these are viewed as ways of spreading the company's message with little effort and minimal expenditure, achieving a positive perspective from consumers resulting in increased momentum for the service offering. Just as the success story of one McDonald's franchise propelled others to invest, momentum provides the impetus to a successful service offering to become even more successful. Momentum, nourished with financial assets, can also create a perspective of success for a once-stagnant service offering.

To bring a service offering back to vibrant life typically requires two "momentum" plans. One involves revitalization of the offering—or at least a repackaging to create a new perception. The other is to communicate the story of a revitalized service offering. The following are examples of these plans.

The "development plan" to revitalize the service offering should be tied to the communication or "marketing plan." Each needs to work in synchronization or phases with the other, focusing constantly on creating and supporting service success (or the perception thereof).

Let's use the example of Chrysler to shed light on

the various phases of development:

> *Phase I.* Admit that your service needs improve-
> ment. Chrysler's Lee Iacocca used this technique
> shortly after he assumed the company's helm.
> Basically, Iacocca, as spokesperson, said, "We
> have problems; we're going to fix them with help
> (Federal government loans and restructuring) and
> we'll be back, better than ever."

> *Phase II.* Commit resources (financial and person-
> nel) to fixing the problem. Again, in Chrysler's
> case, refinancing, restructuring, new design, and
> major human-resource commitments were under-
> taken.

> *Phase III.* Introduce the revitalized or new ser-
> vices. For Chrysler, this included offering new
> warranties, new low-rate financing, rebates and,
> of course, new car models.

Another example of an equally difficult dead-end
situation that was turned around through a phased
plan was Harley-Davidson, which went from declin-
ing market share and lost revenue back to product
superiority and financial strength. In essence, the plan
rolled the offering progressively upward from the
stage of admitting a problem to the "corrected" stage,
wherein the firm is perceived to be healthier and more
vibrant.

But this is only half of the "momentum" solution.
The other half, and equally, if not more important
today, is the "marketing plan." This plan, which can
also be phased in, is as follows:

Phase I. This parallels Phase I of the development plan in that it establishes the perception of a base (bottom) in the initial announcement: "We're not the best, but we're going to be." A safer approach for those who do not have the stomach to make this admission is simply to proceed with a safe campaign until they are ready for Phase II. A safe campaign is one in which nothing is promised or actually done. Instead the communication tends to be symbolic, e.g., the company's logo or name superimposed against a sunset.

Phase II. This also runs in sync with the development plan. In this case, the marketing plan goes from the static recognition/statement phase to a dynamic demonstration of the motion/momentum in progress. For Chrysler it was a depiction of the assembly line with Lee Iacocca proclaiming, "We're building them better—we're changing (for the better) for America." Most service businesses that have invested in refurbishing the product or in rejuvenating the service offering have utilized this phase in their marketing. In this phase we often hear such catch phrases as, "We're changing"; "We're getting ready"; "Watch us."

Phase III. This is synonymous with its counterpart in the development plan. Most often the word "new" is used: "Forget the past, we're new and watch us now."

Going beyond the *points of encounter* is what ways-and-means momentum plans are all about. People want to be perceived as intelligent consumers. If the development and marketing plans for momentum convey the impression of enough momentum, the cynical consumer will give you a try. And, if the ten steps to service success have been followed, and you are fulfilling at the *points of encounter*, you are on your way to winning.

Just as there are perceptions you can create (through such offerings as those "extras"), there are "signals" your message sends to the consumer. In today's cynical consumer marketplace, these "descriptives" have taken on a different meaning from those used traditionally in the 1960s, the 1970s or even the 1980s. While there are no sure-fire selections without pre-testing, there are a number of ways to view descriptives. The following illustration demonstrates this "change in meaning."

PERSPECTIVE

Descriptive	*Traditional*	*Cynical*
New	Improved	Repackaged
Dependable	Reliable	Old
Value	Good Price	Quality Sacrificed
Top	Best	One of Many

SIGNAL

Static Descriptives	*Dynamic Descriptives*
Depend	Reflect
Clean	New
Improved	Changed
Quality	Excellence
Traditional	Today's

Further, descriptives also send signals based on *how* they are used and, likewise, if there has been a shift in the signal sent. Some can be categorized as "signals of life" (dynamic) and others as "signals of death" (static).

In today's environment, static descriptives are not only signals of stagnation, they destroy momentum. They negate the connotation of a renewed service offering.

On the other hand, dynamic descriptives are momentum movers. The dynamic descriptives connote an active state of mind reflective of the changing consumer. Use of these dynamic descriptives leaves less room for cynical challenge. For example, the cynical consumer is conditioned to challenge the word "clean" by looking for the dirty. On the other hand, it is difficult to challenge the word "reflect" as it mirrors one's thoughts or tastes.

Sounds complex but it's not. Cynical consumers tune out the real meanings of words such as: "depend," "quality," and "traditional." These static descriptives have been overused and have lost their purity of meaning.

Think about these two insurance company pitches to the same cynical consumer. Allstate says if you buy their insurance, "You are in good hands; you can depend on us." Teachers Insurance says if you buy their "MOD" policy, "you can tailor it to your needs." Simply stated, to the former pitch, the cynical consumer asks: Shouldn't all insurance companies be dependable? However, in the latter case, consumers react positively to the concept of "tailoring it" themselves. How can you react negatively to yourself? Use of the dynamic descriptives opens a clear communications path to overcoming consumer cynicism.

Verbiage vs. Substance

Many firms in the 90s have jumped on the "total commitment to quality" bandwagon. The advertising messages are full of phrases like "service excellence," and "commitment to quality." The consumer expectation is that these firms will fulfill with the exceptional effort, not the ordinary. Have these firms developed substance behind the verbiage? Are there visible or tangible signals directed to the customer that say "here is what we promised *and* here is more"? This will signal real satisfaction. Winning repeat patronage is extremely important in the marketplace full of new competitors and special "try me" offers. Here are some things that can be done to go from verbiage to substance:

> I. *Identify what you already do right.* It may be as simple as placing an appropriate sticker on a service you're already providing. For example, "This container has been packed with care, or "We've taken special care to assure your arrangements are to your specific instructions." Walk through your delivery process and you will, in all likelihood, find many areas where you are already providing service excellence. Label these as such. You can't lose.

> II. *Review what else can be added to distinguish your service offering.* Can you add a tangible or visible

signal to the customer that supports your "service excellence"? Simple tangibles, like a bowl of fruit in a reception area, complimentary champagne or beverage, or chocolate mints, will create a perception change in the customer. Don't forget to connect these "substance" steps to your message about commitment to quality and service excellence with an identifier phrase, card or packaging.

III. Assess the level of personal involvement. There are very few tangible and visible substitutes for human involvement and the higher the level of management involved with the customer, the greater the customer's perception of caring and commitment. Are your managers locked in an office, pushing papers, or behind a glass wall? Shouldn't they be on their feet, smiling, greeting, thanking, resolving problems, and interfacing with the customer?

These three simple steps will take you from "verbiage" to "substance," change the perception of your service offering and give you a differentiating competitive edge. Use these steps to give your customers a true "win" signal and when that happens— you can't lose.

Undermining Service Success

In today's service industry, other offerings can have an impact—directly or indirectly. For example, many firms enlist telemarketing services to solicit additional business, or contract with outside companies to handle complaints. Who then, becomes your first *point-of-encounter* contact with that potential customer? And who becomes your potentially last contact point with your existing customer? Someone who is not even on your direct payroll!

How many times have you been solicited over the telephone by a person with whom you were not particularly pleased? And didn't displeasure reflect on the product or service being offered? How do you feel when someone says, "Let me get that information and pass it along to someone with the company?" These simple examples of a successful operation being undermined by being sandwiched between contracted services.

Question: How would you feel if you were a customer of a fast-food establishment and the touch pad cash register total was more than the actual cost? You wouldn't know, nor would you care, that the Cash Register Service Company is only the supplier. All you would care about is that you were overcharged by the fast-food outlet and, maybe even worse, suspect it was intentional since "the machine did it."

Simply stated, when you strive for a successful offering, your steps must take you beyond even the logical *points of encounter*. What kind of impression do you think your valued customers would have if, on July 15th, they received a letter such as the following from your contracted direct-mail house?

Dear Valued Customer:
    You have been a steady purchaser of our

services. We have grown to know your needs and have tried to meet them in every way possible. To show our appreciation for your loyal patronage and continued use of our services, we have a win-win offer for you.

First, the enclosed credit check gives you $100 toward any service offering you desire. Second, we are reducing prices on all service offerings 50% during valued-customer days. So, join us for this very special thank you to our valued customers.

Sincerely,
Your Service for Success Company

P.S. The special $100 credit check and 50% discount are valid on "valued customer days—July 1–3" at all of our convenient service centers.

Sure, you could fire the contracted firm and repeat the offer, but if you had applied the ten steps to service success to all your *points of encounter*, including those contracted, you would have avoided the damaging undermining effect. Also, whether you conduct your own shoppers service or hire another firm to check other *points of encounter*, you must remember to place your own name (or the name of someone you can trust) on your lists in a distinctly identifiable way. If you should receive mail with the identifiable label you'll know that the outside contracted service has sold your customer list to a competitor.

Conclusion

Service success occurs when the *points of encounter* are well managed. Today's savvy consumer responds to provable perceptions and real people. The enhancement of your service offering won't be helped in the executive suite. It will be helped if those in the executive suites concentrate on ensuring that the right field generals and *point-of-encounter* employees are in place. And make sure that those field generals project the image and actions of a congenial quarterback. Then, look for—and support—your *point-of-encounter* employees who go that step beyond in striving to let the customer win.

You can't lose if the customer wins!

V

The Winners
at Service
Success

Today's winners are those who overcome consumer cynicism by exceeding expectations and going beyond the *point of encounter*. These firms are successful because they have invested for the long term through recognizing that service fulfillment not only promotes growth of their customer base, but retains customer loyalty. While undoubtedly many such firms could be included by a study of their sales growth, the following is a list of some of the "best" or "winners" in their field. To be included, the companies had to be in business two or more years; their products or services are distinguished by notable consumer acceptance; they have overcome prior consumer cynicism; and they have gone beyond the *point of encounter* to be more successful than their competition.

In seeking to identify those firms that represent winners at service success, some common factors emerge. First, each firm understands the customer's perspective and knows how to communicate effectively. Each gives visible signals that tell the consumer, "We want to convert you to a loyal customer through our actions." Each anticipates problems and has developed systems of response. Each recognizes the need to recruit, train, and retrain personnel. And finally, each recognizes the specific needs of the market and has developed a value-added aspect to its service.

There are many losers as well, and such a list would be long indeed. To such firms, I recommend the application of the ten steps and studying these winners at service success.

American Express—for the Gold Card
The recently implemented, detailed monthly statements, complete with photocopy of actual

charges that are further enhanced by the year-end expenditure analysis, is an accountant's dream come true. More importantly, the "let the customer feel good" attitude practiced by company service representatives reflects state-of-the-art training; response time reflects state-of-the-art technology. American Express membership *does* have its privileges.

AMICA Mutual Insurance Co.—Customer Service Representatives
Let's face it. Between the heavy volume of mail, telephone calls, and pushy direct-sales efforts, most people view insurance companies in the same light as the IRS—a necessary evil. It is, therefore, a rarity that a company such as AMICA emerges as a service company worth recognizing. AMICA customer service representatives work for you, with you, and *without* hassling you. The billings are clear and offer flexible payment options. Dividend returns are always pleasant surprises and when making additional service offerings available, their approach is most subtle. In this crowded market sector, AMICA is truly a "mutual association." You're actually their partner—not someone to be milked for more.

AMR—Sabre Reservations System
Serving virtually everyone touched by the travel industry—travel agents, consumers, and businesses of every size and scope—the Sabre System and AMR are standouts. Their own reservationists are among the best in the industry, and the physical product is continually improving. AMR provides superior services to its customers

through ongoing staff training, system enhancement, and user conferences second to none. Everything from boarding passes and seat assignments to bonus miles are provided to customers of American Airlines.

AT&T—Call Waiting and Call Forwarding

AT&T's relatively new at-home services quite possibly may have been responsible for saving many business deals, avoiding personal misfortune, and even saving lives. Think of the call that came through on Call Waiting from the child who missed the school bus and was stranded and the many other urgent messages. This is an unobtrusive at-home service now available as a result of technological development. Yes, AT&T is still tops for service when needed. Of course, we should not fail to mention the high quality of their telephones and backed by their service stores, especially when compared with cheap plastic imitations, backed only by cardboard.

Delta Airlines—Customer Service Personnel

This is a textbook example that states the case for careful recruiting, thorough training, and assignment of appropriate staff, which meld to form a professional team. Highly visible by their red jackets, Delta's personnel efficiently, effectively, and almost always with warm sincerity, handle unsure senior citizens, uptight business executives, and children excited or upset at the prospect of airline travel. They accomplish this with a smile, a friendly word, and even a hand hold. When Delta says it "cares" you can believe it does. This caring is reflected in their customer-contact people, who are able to perceive the need to go beyond that critical initial *point of encounter.*

Federal Express—For Year-After-Year Consistency
The year 1988 marked a 15-year milestone for this company, which has been written up as virtually every critic's choice. They absolutely, positively *do* get it there overnight. The user/consumer-friendly system not only works, it has become addictive; just ask any company controller. This ideal-for-the-procrastinator service is also blessed with thoroughly trained personnel and supported by a computer information system that is just short of miraculous.

Fidelity Investments—"T" Master Account
Many have tried, but few have achieved the goal of putting it all together in a format that the consumer can understand at first glance. The "T" Master Account statement provides an easy-to-use summary of the many fine investment choices offered by the Fidelity Investments supermarket of funds. This is a service firm that has communicated with its information systems (computer) people so that they make not only "cents" but "sense."

FTD—Florists That Deliver
Flower Telegraph Delivery continues to provide a reliable floral delivery network that is accessible from home or office. Materials provided by FTD to member florists include catalogs, actual displays, and how-to materials, for consistency of product delivery as well as service to con-

sumer and recipient. Multiple pricing options and speedy delivery systems provide additional services resulting in enhanced overall sales for member florists and increased value to clientele. So, let's say it with flowers—a bouquet to FTD for going way beyond the *point of encounter*!

Hertz—For the Hertz Platinum Service
Speaking as one of the fortunate few thousand who have been invited by Hertz to carry their Platinum Card, I say, "Thank you!" This unique service deserves special recognition for its superior training of staff, *point-of-encounter* execution, and the extraordinary benefits provided to users. Hertz's accomplishments are all the more noteworthy considering the difficulties inherent in the nature of the service offering. Hertz—with this service—you *are* Number One!

IBM—Word Processors and Office-Related Services
Revamping the secretarial function, with its related behavioral changes, has been no easy task. Introduction of word processing has raised the technical skills required and with it the potential for greatly increased production in a variety of new functions and responsibilities. Since equipment downtime has the potential for paralyzing production, it quickly became obvious to IBM that service and information support after the sale was absolutely essential to continued company growth. In addition to its new products and innovations, IBM provides both local and national (toll-free numbers) access to service and informa-

tion support via on-call representatives. The company's product guarantees and replacement procedures successfully convey to the end-user a "we" attitude. When it comes to problem resolution, even though there are companies that clone IBM's machines, they can't clone their service support network.

Marriott—Hotels and Resorts
This is a company that executes the ten steps to service success as well as any. Masters at recruiting and training bright, energetic people, Marriott's communications go both ways, and usually result in improved service. There are competitors who use the expression "cookie cutter" to describe the Marriott product; however, customers see it as representing consistency and quality of service. The three Rs of Marriott are "Research, Reassessment, and Reallocation." And Marriott gets a triple "A" rating for follow-up.

McDonald's—Fast-food Service
There are times when systems, procedures, and training are enough to make a difference. But if you add to these a product that meets a need and a quick, convenient delivery system, you have a winner. Add a people-pleasing menu, the convenience of drive-through service, free refills of coffee for seniors, quality packaging and promotions that kids love, and you have a classic success story. Because the offerings are so attractive, people line up, but they are handled quickly; and isn't it worth the wait? McDonald's University, quality control, and systems that work all add up to a service success!

Mercedes—Dealerships Across American and Elsewhere

Clean, precise, trained, and professional are all adjectives that aptly describe the Mercedes operation. Going beyond the *points of encounter*, the customer can experience a superior "loaner" program and limousine pick-up and drop-off service. I know of a dealer whose customers' cars are picked up for service even though they are more than 20 miles away. Repairs are done right the first time. Demanding—even rude—customers are handled diplomatically by employees who are trained to please these car owners. Mercedes not only sets the standards for production of luxury vehicles but, more importantly, the *service* standards.

Midas—More Than Mufflers

Midas's service translates to convenience, quality, and no-nonsense guarantees. The parts are available, as is the system to provide quick service for the most discerning customer. Midas stays open until that 5:45 P.M. last-minute job is completed. There are no hassles, no hidden work areas, and no hidden costs—all of which add up to service satisfaction.

3-M—Technical Service System

This is a triple-win system. First, equipment comes with an easy-to-read "fix it yourself" service manual. Second, a toll-free number provides reliable instructions and advice; 3-M guarantees that a technician will call back within 60 minutes. Third, if that doesn't solve the problem, a technician will be on the way. You can use one of their convenient yellow Post-It pads to keep that toll-free number handy!

The Sharper Image—Stores Across America and Catalogs, too!
Attractive stores, quality merchandise, eye-pleasing displays, and well-trained employees all add up to service success. Employees display great tact in responding to even the most inane inquiries; they know their product line and aren't pushy in making sales. Returns are seldom a problem and the quality of merchandise reflects the demands of their customers. The Sharper Image is sharp indeed in maintaining a sharp service image!

Stouffer Hotels and Resorts—Morning Coffee and Newspaper Service
Stouffer says its product and service are a tradition. But to become a tradition with meaning, one must be consistent in providing excellent service. Wake-up calls are made by personable people (not recordings), and morning coffee (or tea) is served in real china on a lined tray—with the morning paper. Service is prompt.

Society National Bank—Private Banking Service
Remember the "good old days" when the same person gave you and your account personal attention—someone to whom you were not just a number? Well, in Cleveland, Ohio, you can still get such service from the "Personal Banking Service" of Society National Bank. The personnel are well trained, not only in financial matters, but in

human relationships. Adjectives such as "warm," "flexible," "friendly," and "helpful" aptly describe their offering. All customers are given quick service and are treated with respect. In addition, the interest rates are always among the best in the nation.

Walt Disney Companies—From the Magic Kingdom to motion pictures
A prime example of the "ten steps to service success" at work can be found in virtually all of the Walt Disney operations. Excellent recruitment, training, communication, research—and problem recognition with effective solutions—are all prevalent in the Disney organization.

Xerox—for the Xerox Telecopier and User Training
There is always someone with a better way of doing it. So Xerox came up with its telecopier. For quick and efficient document transmission, the Xerox telecopier surpasses next-day/overnight or same-day service. It is accomplished in the time it takes to place a telephone call. User training is provided at installation, with help available upon request.

Office staffs have quickly recognized the benefits of this effective and economical method of information transfer.

While I have highlighted these 20 firms who have gone beyond the point of encounter with their service or product offerings, there are others that deserve recognition for outstanding performance:

Avis—"Research and Development" leader in the rent-a-car industry, from the "Wizard: to Rapid Check-In, this firm truly reflects a caring owner-ship—its employees!

CNN—Its objective research and communication of important issues has tended to reduce viewer cynicism.

Consumer Reports—its unbiased presentation of important facts and figures is based on careful research and is presented in a clear and usable style.

Dunkin' Donuts—Franchisee-training at Donut University is required by all, regardless of wealth. It pays off with consistent fresh products and prompt service across America.

Forbes—It gives its readers more research, and more coverage of significant facts and figures—the Forbes "500."

Frequent Flyer/Pocket OAG—It provides the frequent flyer traveler with up-to-date information.

H&R Block—It provides thousands of Americans with a simple solution to an increasingly complex problem of understanding and filing tax returns.

New York Times, Sunday edition—It provides so much to its readers beside the news—facts, insights, book reviews, fashion, finance, the arts, and sports—and is delivered so widely.

Nordstroms—Its department stores exemplify application of the ten steps and also go beyond the *point-of-encounter*.

Pennzoil—Its instant lube centers demonstrate how research really pays off. Their ten-minute oil change system provides a needed service to millions.

Rouse Company—It is a master planner that applies all ten steps in revitalizing cities for their inhabitants and visitors (for example, Harborplace in Baltimore), proving that urban renewal is alive and well.

Sears—It is dedicated to offering a wide variety of home services and pays attention to customer service at the store level.

SOHIO Procare—It, too, recognized a need, researched the market, reallocated resources, and communicated its convenient service ("leave your car for repair and cleaning while you travel") to the marketplace.

Stanley Steamer—It convinced even service personnel that it passes the "white towel" test. It offers a complete cleaning service that works.

Swissair—It is a master of providing air service, always efficient and dedicated to quality. It follows the ten steps to success.

Toyota Lexus—This new luxury car and its sparkling dealership and service network bring new meaning to automobile quality and service excellence.

The Weather Channel—It recruits the best meteorologists to monitor the world's weather and makes the information available on a daily (even hourly) basis. It doesn't just report the weather; it relates it to your needs.

United Parcel Service—It has demonstrated that training and retraining pays off. It runs clean, well-maintained trucks, employs dedicated personnel, and provides service that is reliable.

USA Today—It communicates concise facts with objectivity. Some call it "McPaper" and well they should. It even provides *good* news!

Yankelovich Clancy Shulman—It is a research-and-consulting service that goes beyond the *point of encounter* to actually become a part of the thought-processes of the firms it serves. Over the years it probably has sown the seeds for thousands of new product and service ideas.

In addition to these outstanding firms, special recognition goes to a service group known as the professional certified travel agents. Regardless of travel organization affiliations, today's travel agent makes an outstanding effort to give the public the best available information on the many and confusing air fares, leisure destination choices, and business travel services. In fact, many agencies personify the concept of "value added services" by going beyond the *point of encounter*.

A salute to the travel agents of America would also not be complete without equal recognition to what is referred to as the "bible of the travel planner," Hotel and Travel Index. This publication has improved every year for over 50 years by conducting extensive research among its users and advertisers (the suppliers of travel services). This publication exemplifies the first and tenth steps of service success by constantly seeking to understand its customers' perspective and by "starting over again" each year to do even better.

Whether or not they are in the Forbes "500," these firms share many common elements that add up to service success and, in one way or another, have gone beyond the *point of encounter.*

INDEX

ABOUT THE AUTHOR

Ronald A. Nykiel is senior marketing officer for Stouffer Hotels and Resorts, a Nestle company. His business career includes IBM, Xerox, and Marriott corporations.

Dr. Nykiel has consulted for two presidential commissions and for leading service industry-related firms. He has lectured at Harvard Graduate School of Business and other universities on the subjects of marketing, consumer behavior, executive development, and corporate strategy. Dr. Nykiel holds a Ph.D. in Behavioral Studies.